BRIDGING SOCIAL AND GEOGRAPHICAL SPACE THROUGH NETWORKS

BRIDGING SOCIAL AND GEOGRAPHICAL SPACE THROUGH NETWORKS

edited by
HELEN DAWSON
& FRANCESCO IACONO

© 2021 Individual authors

Published by Sidestone Press, Leiden
www.sidestone.com

Imprint: Sidestone Press Academics

Lay-out & cover design: Sidestone Press
Photograph cover:
- Copy of the "sala", the traditional lofting floor of the Mavrikos brothers, Syros, Greece. Photo: Kostas Damianidis, Courtesy of the Museum of the Aegean Boatbuilding and Maritime Crafts, Samos, Greece.

ISBN 978-94-6427-000-6 (softcover)
ISBN 978-94-6427-001-3 (hardcover)
ISBN 978-94-6427-002-0 (PDF e-book)

Published with funding from the Gerda Henkel Stiftung, Düsseldorf

Contents

About the authors   7

Bridging Social and Geographical Space through Networks: Introduction   9
    Helen Dawson and Francesco Iacono

Three simple geographical network models for the Holocene Bismarck Sea   15
    Mark Golitko and John Edward Terrell

Terrestrial Transportation Networks and Power Balance in Etruria and Latium Vetus between the beginning of the Early Iron Age and the end of the Archaic Period   31
    Francesca Fulminante, Alessandro Guidi, Sergi Lozano, Ignacio Morer, Luce Prignano

Getting around the city: A Space Syntax perspective on post-medieval Nuremberg   47
    Donat Wehner

Memory as a network of affects: Bridging the humanities and social sciences to understand the social spaces of storytelling   59
    Sarah De Nardi

At the heart of *Mare Nostrum:* Islands and "small world networks" in the central Mediterranean Bronze Age   71
    Helen Dawson

Marx, networks and the social logic of interaction   89
    Francesco Iacono

Bibliography   103

About the authors

Helen Dawson is Adjunct Professor at the Department of History, Cultures and Civilisations at the University of Bologna and affiliate Research Fellow at the Institute of Prehistory of the Freie Universität Berlin. At the time of writing, she was Gerda Henkel Research Fellow in Archaeology at the Topoi Excellence Cluster, FU Berlin. She is the author of "Mediterranean Voyages. The Archaeology of Island Colonisation and Abandonment" (Left Coast Press/Routledge, 2014). Her research focuses on understanding different forms of colonisation, island networks, and the recursive relations shaping human practices and insularity.

Sarah De Nardi is Lecturer in Heritage and Tourism at Western Sydney University. She is the author of "The Poetics of Conflict Experience. Materiality and Embodiment in Second World War Italy" (Routledge, 2016). Her book revived the poetics of landscape and conflict perception in Second World War Italy through the prism of materiality, contemporary identity politics, memory, and embodiment. She is also the editor-in-chief of the forthcoming "Routledge Handbook of Memory and Place" and of the "Routledge Handbook of Community Archaeology".

Francesca Fulminante has recently completed a Marie Curie Sklodowska Fellowship (University of Roma Tre). Her research and teaching focuses mainly on urbanization in central Italy, both as a socio-political and economic process (settlement organization, networks and interactions and textile tools from surveys, within the PROCON project), and on its relation to more intimate aspects such as infancy and motherhood.

Mark Golitko is an Assistant Professor in the Department of Anthropology at University of Notre Dame. A specialist in applications of the physical sciences and network analysis to archaeological research, his current field research explores the development of social networks and bio-cultural diversity on the north coast of Papua New Guinea during the last 6000 years as climate, environment, and technology underwent dramatic changes. He has also carried out field and laboratory research on the archaeology of Europe, Mesoamerica, and South America.

Alessandro Guidi is Full Professor of Prehistoric and Protohistoric Archaeology at Roma Tre University. His research focuses on the proto-history of the Italian peninsula, particularly the birth of the city and the state, the history of prehistoric studies, and theoretical archaeology and methodology. Some of his key publications include "History of Palethnology" (1988), "The methods of archaeological research" (1994, 2005), and "Prehistory of social complexity" (2000). He has conducted excavations, surveys and research activities in Italy, Hungary and Russia participating in congresses and lecturing in Europe, India and the United States.

Francesco Iacono is Senior Assistant Professor in Prehistory at the Department of History, Cultures and Civilisations at the University of Bologna. His research interests range from prehistory and archaeology of the Mediterranean (with particular attention to the Bronze Age), to social theory (in particular Marxist archaeology) to the use of applications based on graph-theory, to cultural heritage studies, and, finally, the history of the archaeological thought.

Sergi Lozano is 'Ramón y Cajal' (tenure-track) Research Fellow at the Institut Català de Paleoecologia Humana i Evolució Social (IPHES). He holds a Degree in Engineering and a PhD in Sustainability Science. His research has mainly focused on complex networks and techno-social systems. Dr. Lozano's current interests include long-term social and cultural phenomena from the Human Past.

Ignacio Morer is an Industrial Engineer from Universidad de Zaragoza. He holds a Master's Degree in Mathematical Modelling, Statistics and Computation and recently started his PhD at Universitat de Barcelona – CLabB, within the EPNet Project. His research interests are mainly related to complex networks analysis, specifically in the archaeological and social context.

Luce Prignano received her degree in Physics (2005) and MSc in "Theoretical Physics – Statistical Physics curriculum" (2008) from the University "Sapienza" of Rome and her PhD (2012) in Physics from Barcelona University. During her pre-doctoral stage, her research focused mainly on the interdependence between dynamic properties and topology of complex networks (especially emerging phenomena such as synchronisation). Between 2013 and 2015, she was a postdoctoral researcher at IPHES in the COMPATHEVOL research group.

John Edward Terrell is Regenstein Curator of Pacific Anthropology at the Field Museum of Natural History in Chicago. He is also a professor of Anthropology at the University of Illinois Chicago and an adjunct professor of Anthropology at Northwestern University. He has written extensively about the spatial, geographical, psychological, and social dimensions of human adaptation and evolution. His recent book summarising many of his major research findings and hypotheses over the course of the last half century is entitled "A Talent for Friendship: Rediscovery of a Remarkable Trait", published by Oxford University Press in December 2014.

Donat Wehner is a Research Fellow of Historical Archaeology at Kiel University. The focus of his research concentrates on the archaeology of the Western Slavs, medieval and post-medieval archaeology as well as computational archaeology.

Bridging Social and Geographical Space through Networks: Introduction

Helen Dawson and Francesco Iacono

Networks, Archaeology, Geography, Social space, Theory, Interdisciplinarity

Networks: A ubiquitous metaphor
Networks of all kinds (social, cultural, religious, economic, political, etc.) underpin our lives and are an obvious way of thinking about social relations. Unsurprisingly, studying networks has become a priority for social scientists, economists, politicians, and philosophers alike. We generally think of archaeologists as being primarily concerned with studying the past but archaeology also provides a bridge between past and present. Global interaction is at its current scale an inherently modern phenomenon but, at different scales, finds valid parallels in the past. How did social interaction work in the past and what can it tell us about how current networks have developed? Conversely, can interaction in the present tell us something about the past? Thinking through networks can make us reconsider how we have conceived of societal change so far, to the point that we may be living through another "cognitive revolution" (Terrell et al. 2014).

Networks have been ubiquitous in our discussions for such a long time that by now we almost take them for granted. From an operational perspective, they are an extremely effective metaphor for explaining the inner workings of communication and social relations, providing formal methods to grapple with the complexities of the way people interact (Barabási 2002; 2010; Castells 1996; White 2008). More broadly, within the field of the humanities, networks offer a number of approaches, comprising both qualitative and quantitative applications. Thanks to the development of network applications in archaeology over the last few years, a number of important insights and overarching concerns have emerged, whose recognition – we believe – will help further the field (Brughmans 2010; 2012; Collar et al. 2015; Mills 2017; Knappett 2013). These insights mostly concern the interface between theory and practice: on the one hand, theoretical concerns arise over the ubiquity of what we define as networks; on the other, the relative ease of applying networks as a methodological approach (which is in no small part responsible for its success) is striking. Both concerns relate to the issue of representation, *i.e.* the dual process of inferring social relations from archaeological data and mapping them into network structures. Many recent studies have attempted to model "reality" through networks using a variety of proxies, ranging from traditional archaeological data (Blake 2014; Iacono 2016; Knappett 2014) to archaeometric data (Radivojević and Grujić 2018), from linguistic data to genetic data (Barbieri et al. 2017; Heggarty 2007). Networks are undoubtedly useful heuristic tools, but what is it we are actually connecting? To what extent do networks approximate "reality"? How does studying interaction allow us to understand better and possibly even redefine what is being connected?

Directly related to this discussion is the difficulty engendered by the different scales and qualities of the phenomena to be represented and reduced to the network dimension (see Dawson infra). While the ability to represent everything through a graph is, as we have highlighted, the very essence of the success of networks in current scholarship, there is an element of reductionism that can be potentially problematic if it is not explicitly addressed. Of course, all archaeological models require a simplification of reality, which is only meaningful if appropriate standards of scientific enquiry are adopted; the same applies to networks.

So far, discussion on this theme has focused on two overarching domains: on the one hand, following parallel developments in social physics and digital humanities, network approaches in archaeology have produced an increasingly refined set of methods which enable us to explore the logic of connection particularly on the large scale (Orengo and Livarda 2016; Prignano et al. 2017). On the other hand, while the allure of "Big Data" is certainly understandable (Bentley et al. 2014), we are equally aware of the shortcomings of this approach, particularly its ineffectiveness in terms of bridging the larger level of analysis with everyday practices at the smaller scale and gauging their social significance. How can we satisfactorily assess the structural or "topological" relations reconstructed from archaeological data if we do not understand what they mean? Researchers adopting a "Big Data" approach even predicted the end of theory, arguing that answers could be derived from data themselves, essentially replacing causation with correlation (Anderson 2008, but see critique by Mazzocchi 2015). Despite this trend, we believe we should always aim to investigate and conceptualise the deeper reasons for complexity and interaction. So for instance, even acknowledging that mobility of people can be classed into different categories, it is difficult to make sense of different mobility patterns without making inferences on the societies producing them.

Social and geographical space: Towards an integrated approach

This volume comprises a seemingly eclectic collection of contributions that were originally presented at a workshop we held in Berlin at the Topoi Excellence Cluster (for the original programme, see here: https://www.topoi.org/event/32715). The topics presented are evidence of the broad range of directions network-based research can take. Despite this conceptual diversity and the consequent variety of potential scientific applications, two main strands in network approaches have emerged in recent years and our workshop and volume clearly reflect this: those centred on spatial analysis and those concerned with the social dimensions of interaction. Methodologically, both spatial and social approaches entail the analysis of relations and their patterning, but the former is grounded in geographic space as intended by a variety of disciplines (including Landscape

Archaeology and Geography, normally analysed through GIS-based approaches and geographic networks). The latter, instead, is more concerned with the analysis of social relations with an emphasis on "topology", *i.e.* the very structure of relations, rather than their physical manifestation (usually approached via social network analysis or other graph-based theoretical approaches in which the spatial dimension is removed).

While these traditions currently comprise separate approaches, with distinct ancestries, within the humanities, we have long been aware of the deep interplay between social and geographical space. Geographers since Lefebvre (2009 [1974]) have been mindful of the social nature of space, a focus that through the mediation of anthropology has been transferred to other historical disciplines. In archaeology, in particular, this focus has led to phenomenological approaches to studying landscapes (Claval 1993; Gregory and Urry 1985; Harvey 1994; Low 1996; Shanks and Tilley 1987; Tilley 1994). In parallel, social theorists, at least from Durkheim onwards, have been adopting some notion of "social space" (Castells 1996; Claval 1984) and relating it to geographical space, albeit in a non-linear fashion. This attention on space within social theory culminated in two distinct trends focusing on the macro and the micro scale respectively. The first, dealing with the 'big picture', resulted in discussions of centrality and the consolidation of the World System Theory approach, especially between the 1970s and 1990s (see Dawson infra; Chase-Dunn and Hall 1997; Frank 1993; Kristiansen 1998; Sherratt 1993a; Wallerstein 1974; Wilkinson et al. 2011). The second, more detail-oriented trend employed quantitative methodologies in order to analyse how space constrained or empowered social relationships, through the use of Space Syntax Analysis (see Wehner infra; Chatford Clark 2007; Cutting 2003; on space syntax see Hillier and Hanson 1984) and Agent Based Modelling (Graham 2006; Graham and Weingart 2015). In parallel (also with the development of phenomenological approaches in archaeology), the focus on the micro scale also stemmed an interest for the social aspects of 'place', and an attention to the emotional or affective side of relationships, the 'human' side of networks, which is often neglected and in which obviously co-presence in space features as a crucial variable sewing together community and individuals (Crouch 2015; De Nardi 2016: 1-17; De Nardi infra).

While geographical networks are often used in an exploratory or predictive manner (*e.g.* Proximal Point Analysis, see Golitko and Terrell infra), considering the potential for interconnections, social networks can be either descriptive or analytical or both, but normally work on connections that have already occurred. This spatial/social dichotomy is to some extent an artefact of the different interests of specialists coming from their respective fields, and yet undoubtedly the highest research potential lies at the intersection between these two perspectives, which – if properly analysed – could change the way we think of networks themselves. Geographical and social space can both be conceptualised at different scales; moreover, connections can take place both synchronously and diachronically, and their development observed over time. Bridging these two dimensions, geographic and social, can shed light not just on past or current networks, but also on their potential future development. It can thus allow us to add a third, temporal, dimension, by considering how the potential for interconnectedness changes over time. It was our stated intention at the workshop to integrate these different approaches, for example by exploring how similar questions could be addressed differently, reflecting on methods and results, or the broader applicability or relevance of a particular approach to a different set of questions. It quickly became apparent at the workshop that formal network analysis (*i.e.* model-based approaches) can come across as being overly reductive or simplistic to researchers who are not familiar with such methodologies; equally, qualitative approaches can sometimes be considered as too abstract and lacking empiricism. Swapping between these approaches helped us frame questions differently and open new angles of enquiry. We encouraged contributors to reflect on the usefulness or otherwise of different methods, to attempt a critique of their own work, and establish a dialogue with each other. Integrating different research directions through networks can help us overcome perceived academic boundaries, a goal we set for this volume. Of course these boundaries remain strong and are not easy to overcome; nonetheless this volume represents a first step in this direction.

Outline of the volume

The papers in this volume explore the relation between geographical and social space and come up with a broad range of solutions to the problem of integrating these two aspects through some very different approaches. Broadly speaking, the first set of three papers (comprising Golitko and Terrell; Fulminante, Guidi, Lozano, Morer and Prignano; and Wehner) takes physical or geographical space as its point of departure and explores, through formal hypothesis-testing and network models, how movement across space results from different social and cultural processes (and vice versa). The authors in the second set (De Nardi; Dawson; and Iacono) adopt a critical and qualitative approach in order to consider different scales of social interaction in space and time. These papers focus on the interplay between social and spatial dimensions of interaction and on their transformative effects on the communities involved, to make points relating respectively to collective memory, shifting centrality and marginality, and class and power relations.

The opening contribution by Golitko and Terrell identifies a good match between simple geographical networks and social factors, specifically population levels and the spread of seafaring innovations. Their spatial models, based on fixed radius and point-proximal analysis, help explain the known obsidian distribution patterns in and around northern New Guinea (c. 6000-3500 BP), which in turn provides a proxy for social interaction. Moreover, these social networks approximate a so-called "small-world" featuring strong ties between geographically close areas and weaker ties between more distant areas. This structure underscores important similarities between neighbouring groups, which they view as part of a relational continuum rather than as bounded entities, contrary to traditional historical narratives in the region they discuss. The paper by Fulminante, Guidi, Lozano, Morer and Prignano is a collaboration between an archaeologist and a team of mathematic engineers and physicists. The authors use formal mathematical modelling to understand networks of transportation and communication to explain a crucial historical development: the rise of Rome. They hypothesise that networks shape the societies they connect and are also shaped by them. In this way, the archaeological record of the second and first millennium BC is mobilised to understand how inter-community connections favoured the emergence of visible processes of power accumulation. An important underlying idea here is that of efficiency, viewed as an organising principle at the macro-scale, an element that network studies have inherited from their ancestry in transportation science (see also Wehner infra and Orengo and Livarda 2016).

The papers by Wehner and De Nardi both consider the relation between space and social interaction, but via a quantitative and qualitative approach respectively. Despite their very different points of departure, they reveal some interesting overlaps in their results and perspectives. Moving from the regional to the local dimension, Wehner uses space syntax as a formal methodology to explore and understand the relational space, materiality and daily life of medieval Nuremberg. Through the use of space syntax, "movement" in and around the city is proven to be an aspect that defies certain rational expectations and choices. Rather, movement can be seen as a tool for promoting social reproduction through embodiment in the physical space. Thus, beyond the specific characteristics of the networks being studied, this paper highlights the crucial importance of the micro-scale emerging more generally within any kind of social "interdependency". De Nardi explores the potential of using networks as a metaphor to understand the web of experiences and memories that hold communities together. She approaches the relations between places, experience, and memory via "affectual" networks: people, places, and things are all tied up in networks whose temporality is not constrained by the duration of human lives but extends into the realm of memory. Memory and identity (directly related concepts) bestow a further dimension to physical space and consequently to the networks. In this sense, the topological concept of "node" ends up having a considerable overlap with the psychological notion of "knot", intended as a special entanglement of people, places, times, and experiences (node and knot are the same word in many romance languages, such as French or Italian). Networks of affect can be explored in a variety of contexts and social articulations. In a sense, De Nardi's paper, which finds parallels between Second World War Italy, post-medieval Britain, and Pakistan in the post-Taliban period, extends these networks of affect to the present place and moment, reaching our readers through her narration.

A novel approach, integrating quantitative and qualitative factors to social interaction, is explored in the paper by Helen Dawson. Dawson uses network analysis to explore "interdependency" and redefine narratives of centrality and marginality in the Mediterranean Bronze Age. Focusing on small island- and coastal communities, her study bridges inter-regional and local scales of analysis, presenting interaction as a "small world" network. In a similar vein to Golitko and Terrell (infra), her work shows that island and coastal communities, and the maritime networks they create, can be better understood through a relational perspective, which treats them as interconnected and not as isolated, marginal, and bounded (Dawson 2020). By integrating networks into more established narratives, such as World System Analysis, her paper attempts to capture the complexity and dynamism of interaction in a less rigid fashion.

Finally, while the combined use of different theoretical perspectives has been recognised as a main strength of network approaches (Mills 2017), applications of network analysis are rarely explicit about their underlying social theories. Network analysis still relies on implicit theoretical agendas, often directly borrowed from sociology and/or social physics. Francesco Iacono focuses on a particular aspect that has been relatively neglected by network applications in archaeology, that of power and social differentiation. He advocates in favour of more open theoretical models, in this case one based on an eclectic mixture of radical social theory, as a way of bringing productive change and usefully directing network perspectives towards similarly neglected issues.

Moving forward

Distinguishing between geographical and social aspects of interaction is important but we would argue that the artificial separation of these two aspects, as often seen in different disciplines of the humanities and social sciences, is counterproductive. We hope that the range of papers presented in this collection will persuade the reader that gauging the mutual effects and relationships between these two aspects is necessary if we are to understand interactions between humans more fully. The range of papers in this volume is evidence of the broad scope of directions network research can take within archaeology and more broadly the humanities, as well as the considerable challenges we face and rewards we may reap when we integrate them. We believe they equally highlight some potential future developments network applications to archaeology, geography, and more broadly historical disciplines, can strive to achieve. These relate to two key aspects:

Socialisation of Space: the ways in which networks of human relationships can contribute to the shaping of space and its perception. A variety of humanities methods can be adopted to explore this dimension, ranging from traditional graph-theoretical methods to humanities-based approaches like ethnography;

Spatially situated Social Networks: The ease of movement typical of our contemporary globalised times, as well as the influence of the internet (the most popular network of all), can lead to the erroneous impression that space is a negligible variable. And yet space and the "territorialisation" of relationships (De Landa 2006) act powerfully. Removing this constraint results in social models that are less realistic or grounded. The kind of constraints or opportunities that geography poses onto networks is as much a piece of the equation as the topological or social structure of networks.

While networks represent a useful metaphor and come with a powerful arsenal of analytical tools, it is important not to forget that human networks are also – sometimes fundamentally – emotional structures creating a sense of relatedness, which can bypass physical borders and divisions but also reinforce the imaginary lines we draw around us.

Acknowledgements

We wish to thank the Topoi Excellence Cluster for generously funding the workshop and the Gerda Henkel Stiftung for covering the costs of the publication. We are grateful to all the authors for their contributions, to the reviewers for their feedback, and to Sidestone Press for their support.

Three simple geographical network models for the Holocene Bismarck Sea

Mark Golitko and John Edward Terrell

New Guinea, Obsidian, Lapita, Outrigger Canoe, Network Analysis, Proximal Point Analysis

Archaeology, geographic space, and social networks

Archaeology has always been concerned with human activity in geographical space, particularly in understanding how and why the distribution of things that find their way into the archaeological record changes over time and space. In his well-known work on the anthropology of ethnicity, Barth (1969: 9) argues that most anthropological reasoning is based on the presumption that people can be meaningfully grouped into types with well-defined boundaries, variously conceptualised as ethnic groups, clans, tribes, or in recent applications of DNA based studies, populations. However analytically convenient such a presumption may be, it is hard to find such tightly circumscribed groups in the real world, which is structured by complex overlapping social ties between individuals and communities. Yet much of archaeological practice remains rooted in a 19th century debate over the role of ethnic migration versus local development to explain the dynamics of the past, one viewed through the lens of monolithic socially and geographically bounded archaeological cultures that serve as agents of action responsible for generating changes in style, technology, gene frequencies, and spoken language.

A relational network perspective, at least in our view, stands in contradistinction to such categorical representations of human biocultural patterning in the past and present – far from living in bounded groups, people both past and present live in variably structured and far-reaching social networks that overlap with but are not the same as socially constructed categories such as ethnicity. Granovetter for instance outlined a distinction between what he calls "strong" and "weak" ties (Granovetter 1973: 1363 – 1368). The former reflect the most frequent and intensive social interactions with close friends, neighbors, associates, and so forth, ones which are responsible for the high degree of clustering evident in human social networks (Newman 2003: 3 – 5). The tightly interconnected cliques that result can constrain the movement of ideas and practices, although in other cases, strong ties can be critical to acquiring some kinds of information, including those that require transmission of complex knowledge that requires a long period to learn (Shi et al. 2007). However, weak ties (reflecting more casual and infrequent contacts) also play a significant role in the spread of new ideas.

Archaeological network analyses rely on inferring ties between places on the landscape in one way or another rather than on directly observing social connections between individual actors, as is the norm in most social network analysis in other applications. Ties are often built using either archaeological assemblage information directly (similarity networks) (Östborn and Gerding 2014: 75 – 76), or by modelling plausible ties using either general structural network principles (Amati et al. 2017; Knappett et al. 2008: 1012 – 1014) or by inferring the social, ecological, or economic motivations behind the formation and maintenance of social bonds (Rautman 1993: 420 – 421). As network analysis has tended to focus on social connections and motivations as basic explanatory mechanisms, geography is only sometimes explicitly considered in social network analysis, including archaeological applications. Yet the realities of space and time are part of most real world social interactions, and numerous studies have shown that geography strongly influences how people shape their social contacts whether in face-to-face interactions or when using other methods of communication (e.g., cellular communication or online social networking platforms) (Onnela et al. 2011: e16939; Leskovec and Horvitz 2014: 161). Consequently, geographic distance can be an informative way to estimate the likelihood that people living in different places may have interacted with one another in the past, although constructing plausible models requires carefully considering how and why potential geographical pathways may have been utilised. In general, we would assume that geographically shorter ties are more likely to be stronger ties, while long distance ties are more likely to be weaker ties, although exceptions likely exist as well.

Figure 1: Map of the circum-Bismarck Sea region of northeastern New Guinea showing locations included in our network models as well as the locations and approximate dating of sourced obsidian assemblages from the region.

In focusing primarily on archaeological spatial/cultural boundaries, we would argue, archaeologists frequently undertheorise the potential importance of weaker ties, which may be in some cases far more important for explaining the dynamics of the past. Here we present a set of simple models of changing patterns of interaction along the fringes of the Bismarck Sea in the southwestern Pacific Ocean as an illustration of the potentials of even very simple geographical network models for querying the archaeological record.

The Holocene Southwestern Pacific

The prehistory of New Guinea and its surrounding archipelagos has largely been viewed through the lens of historical linguistics. Linguists classify the languages spoken in the Pacific into two major groups – the Austronesian family, a relatively well defined set of languages spoken between Madagascar to the west, Taiwan to the North, Rapa Nui to the east, and New Zealand to the south – and Papuan or non-Austronesian languages, a diverse set of largely unrelated languages spoken primarily on the island of New Guinea and nearby archipelagos (East Timor, Halmahera, the Bismarcks, and parts of the Solomon Island chain) (Donohue and Denham 2010:223 – 224).

In what may be labeled the "conventional" view of Pacific prehistory, these linguistic distinctions are seen as reflective of different histories for the people involved – in this case, two ethnolinguistic migrations, one which brought the ancestors of modern day Papuan speakers to New Guinea and its surrounding archipelagos (Near Oceania) some 45-55,000 years ago, and a second some 3500-3300 years ago during which ancestral Austronesian speakers bearing Lapita style ceramics (the earliest ceramic industry in the Pacific, characterized initially by elaborate shell-impressed fineware vessels) swept through the coastal margins of New Guinea before rapidly settling Remote Oceania (Diamond 2000:710; Donohue and Denham 2010: 223 – 224).

The "two migration" model of Pacific prehistory (also referred to as the "fast-train" model) is predicated on the assumption that diversity (linguistic, biological, and cultural) is generated via isolation played out over long periods of time (Terrell et al. 1997: 156). In the Pacific case, a belief that along with Austronesian languages and Lapita pottery, these new migrants established long-distance networks of communication and exchange between their newly established coastal settlements, while Papuan speakers remained largely disconnected from these new Austronesian communities (and from each other) until relatively late in the prehistoric sequence of this part of the world (Kirch 1991: 155; Skoglund 2016: 513).

Primary evidence for intensive inter-community interaction between Lapita-using communities comes from the distribution of obsidian (volcanic glass) from sources on New Britain and in the Admiralty group. Around the time that Lapita ceramics first appeared in the St. Matthias Group (by 3300 BP) and on New Britain (by 3000 BP) (Summerhayes 2004: 148, 2009: 115-117; White 1996: 202), Admiralty Island obsidians were being transported to other island groups in and around New Ireland (Summerhayes 2004: 148), and obsidian mined on New Britain was transported to places as far distant as Borneo to the west and Fiji to the east (Summerhayes 2009: 116-117), an east-west distribution of some 7000km.

In this widely-accepted view of Pacific prehistory, it is only around the time that Lapita ceramics disappear from the archaeological record (between about 2000-1800 BP) that Papuan speaking communities became connected to Austronesian speaking coastal villages and to each other. It has been argued that these inter-language ties formed in the context of an overall contraction in the intensity and geographical distance over which exchange and communication took place (Mialanes et al. 2016:255-256), typically inferred on the basis of both reduction in distance over which particular obsidian varieties like Kutau/Bao were transported, and the development of more regionalized stylistic distributions for ceramics and other material culture (Clark 2000: 153). This postulated contraction after 2000 BP is sometimes attributed to the emergence of specialist producers and middlemen (White 1996:202), for instance the emergence within the last 300-500 years of the kula cycle of the Trobriands (Irwin 1983: 69-71), and regionalized "trade spheres" linked by middlemen like the Siassi (Harding 1967: 3), Mailu (Irwin 1978: 408-410), or Manus (Ambrose 1976: 358).

While this model has always had its critics, new archaeological evidence now suggests that materials, ideas, and practices were being widely transported around the fringes of the Bismarck Sea and between Near Oceania and Island Southeast Asia (ISEA) well prior to the appearance of Lapita ceramics. While New Britain and Admiralty obsidian sources had been exploited far back into the Pleistocene, prior to the mid-Holocene (c. 6000-3500 BP), such material was mostly used locally near the source flows (Summerhayes 2009: 114 – 115). By around 6000 BP, however, distinctive obsidian stemmed tools were being widely transported in New Guinea and the Bismarck Archipelago that were manufactured on New Britain using obsidian from the Willaumez Peninsula and Mopir areas. Similar tools were also being made in the Admiralty Islands out of obsidian from local sources there on Lou and Pam Islands (Torrence et al. 2013: 279). Furthermore, the sharing of stylistic traditions is also evident in the contemporaneous wide-spread production and use (and possibly transport) of decorated stone mortars and pestles (Torrence and Swadling 2008: 604 – 605).

White has argued that variable and wide ranging obsidian distribution networks may have been characteristic of the post-Lapita period as well, even if voyaging became the prerogative of only particular communities (White 1996: 205). For instance, obsidian from Fergusson Island (in the Massim/Papuan tip region to the southeast of the area shown in Figure 1) which was principally transported along the south coast of New Guinea occasionally also reached as far north as Seleo Island near Aitape, a distance of more than 1000 km (Golitko et al. 2012: 154 – 155).

Whether contractions and expansions in the distribution of obsidian from particular geologic sources reflect real increases or decreases in inter-community travel and the scope and nature of social ties implied remains uncertain – there are a variety of network structures that might account for the distribution of obsidian, but to date, little formal modelling of these potential structures has been undertaken (White 1996: 203). Here, we apply geographic based network modelling to explore what changes in network topology might account for chronological variation in obsidian distribution during prehistory along the fringes of the Bismarck Sea, and what can be inferred on the basis of transported material culture about the prehistory of the SW Pacific.

Hypotheses and models

To construct networks based on real world geography, we must (a) choose relevant nodes (b) calculate distances between them, and (c) decide which of these geographical routes were possible or likely to have been traversed during the past. Nodes can be placed on actual known archaeological sites, but because we have imperfect knowledge of where settlements may have been located in the past, doing so would likely omit areas of significant settlement density. Instead, we began modelling interaction around the Bismarck Sea by placing nodes in places we suspect once had significant prehistoric settlement, including all major islands or island groups in the study area, as well as mainland areas with larger coastal flats (Fig. 1) (Broodbank 2000: 181-183; Terrell 1974). Some of these places have known archaeological sites, but many have yet to be archaeologically investigated.

While we could incorporate other variables that might have impacted the likelihood of direct travel between any two places, including temporally varying population levels and distributions, changes in coastal morphology resulting from sea-level fluctuation and tectonic forces (influencing both travel distances and population distribution), and changes in wind and current patterns including variability in El Ninõ-Southern Oscillation (ENSO) frequency (influencing speed and possibility of travel in particular directions) (Anderson et al. 2006: 3 – 4), we chose to start simple and constructed a pairwise matrix of geodesic distances between these nodes using latitude and longitude data. We realize, however that it would be unrealistic to assume that each of the resulting ties was equally utilized at all times during the past.

We then built three models by selectively removing geographical ties based on a series of archaeological based scenarios for changes in potential customary voyaging and interaction patterns. These models respectively relate to the period before 3500 BP (Period 1, which largely comprises mid-Holocene age assemblages including isolated finds of stemmed tools), the period contemporary with the production and use of Lapita ceramics in the region (Period 2, c. 3500-2000 BP), and the post-Lapita period (Period 3, c. 2000 BP-100 BP).

Prehistoric Scenarios

Period 1 (~6000-3500 BP): On present evidence, maritime connections across the Bismarck Sea principally developed after 6000 BP, however, individual journeys were potentially limited by extant canoe technology, which was limited to paddled dugouts. During the Pleistocene and early Holocene, longer-distance connections, while feasible given locally available maritime skills and technologies at that time, were restricted by limited coastal population levels (Terrell 2004: 605). The few people living along the coastlines of the Bismarck Sea then were likely mobile foragers (Summerhayes et al. 2017), and travelling longer distances than necessary may have been unappealing given the low likelihood of encountering anyone.

However, after about 6000 BP, stabilization of sea-levels and the consequent development of productive coastal ecosystems after the mid-Holocene marine high stand (Gosden 1995: 809; Terrell 2002: 206 – 207), as well as the spread of highland New Guinea crops like taro (Swadling 2004: 160) and banana (Donohue and Denham 2010: 236), likely fueled rapid population growth and led to more permanent settlement of coastal regions that facilitated the development of wide-reaching maritime-focused social networks through which obsidian and other materials and practices were transported. Coastal voyaging during this period may have been undertaken using paddled canoes like those used for shorter inter-island and near coastal voyages in recent times (Terrell 1986: 137).

Period 2 (~3500-2000 BP): After about 3500 BP, outrigger canoes with Oceanic sprit-sails and associated sailing knowledge were first introduced into the Western Pacific (Terrell 1986: 78 – 79), probably from Island South East Asia or Wallacea (Donohue and Denham 2010: 238), supplanting paddled canoes as the primary means of longer-distance maritime

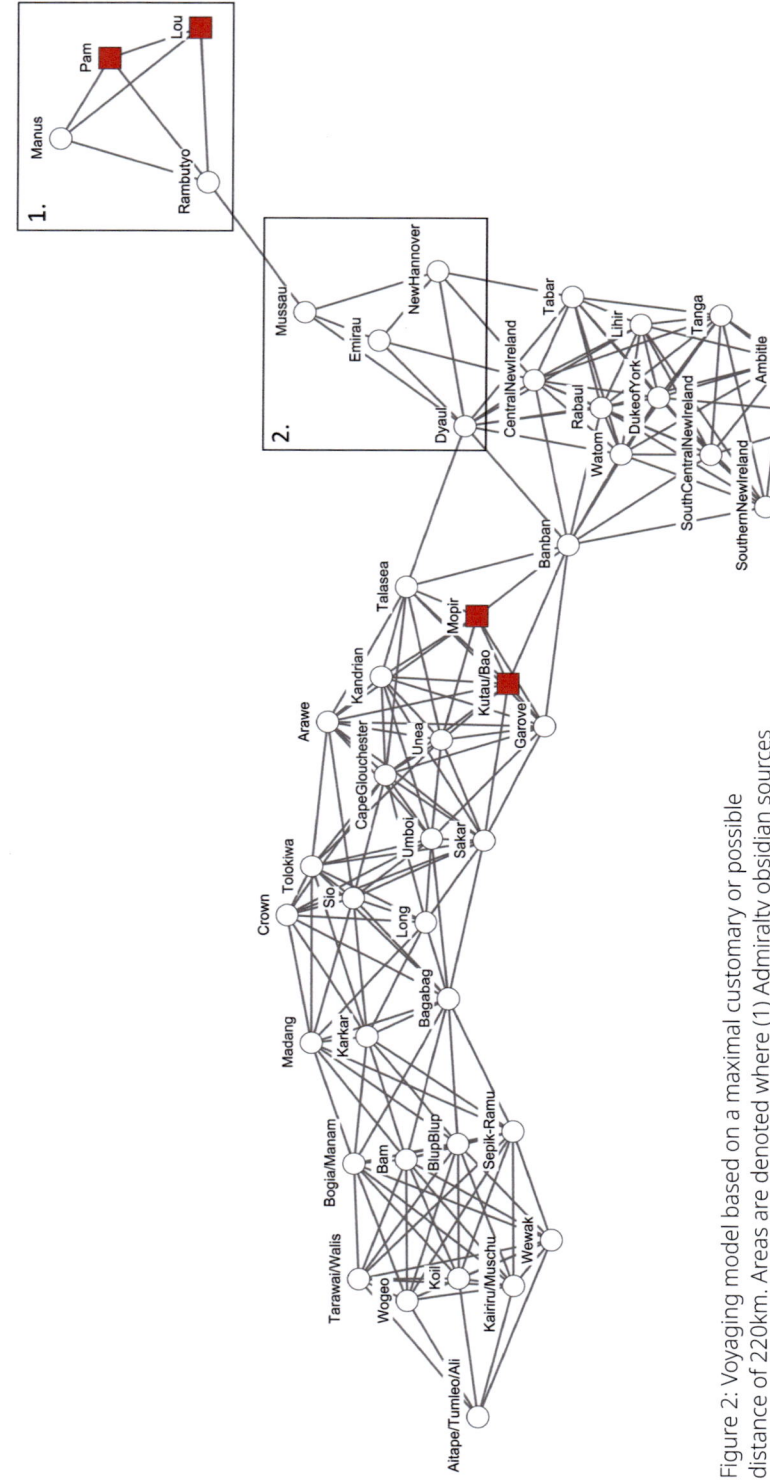

Figure 2: Voyaging model based on a maximal customary or possible distance of 220km. Areas are denoted where (1) Admiralty obsidian sources are most network proximal and (2) Admiralty and New Britain sources are approximately network equidistant. In the rest of the network, New Britain obsidian sources are most proximate to network nodes.

transport. Whether or not all communities acquired outriggers, the introduction of sailing canoes facilitated the development of longer distance connections between communities.

Period 3 (~2000-100 BP): After about 2000 BP, longer distance voyaging increasingly became the social prerogative of people living on a handful of small, relatively resource poor islands, where inhabitants were motivated to maintain social ties that allowed them, among other things, access to mainland foodstuffs (Harding 1994: 108). Most social ties were consequently relatively local, although the inhabitants of areas with few proximal neighbors may have been more motivated to maintain longer-distance ties than those living in densely populated places.

Based on these admittedly simple scenarios, we attempt to construct three models encapsulating the potential impacts of limitations to both geographical and social voyaging distances implied for each prehistoric period, based on filtering a complete matrix of inter-site geodesic distances by a set of particular criteria.

Model I (Period 1, 220 km threshold)

Our first model (Figure 2) assumes only that the maximal likely distance travelled between any two places in this region of the Pacific is 220km or less, but that under the 220km threshold, travel in either direction is equally feasible. This distance value was chosen as it approximates the longest known inter-island distance crossed during the Pleistocene and early to mid-Holocene periods (i.e., pre-3500 BP) now archaeologically documented: specifically the distance between Karkar Island and Manus (assuming lowered sea-levels and larger land areas than at present – at modern sea-levels, that particular inter-island trip is no longer possible at the 220km threshold) (Irwin 1992: 20 – 21).

Model II (Period 2, 360 km threshold)

Model II (Figure 3) was constructed following the same principles as Model I, but it uses a 360km distance threshold, the maximal known inter-island distance crossed during the early colonization of Remote Oceania (from Makiri-Ulawa in the Solomon Island to Temotu in the Reefs/Santa Cruz group). We choose this particular voyage to approximate the sailing capabilities of Pacific Islanders during the earliest introduction of the outrigger canoe into the region (Irwin 1992:20 – 21). Again, most of the ties included in the model are much shorter than 360km and were likely also more frequently traversed than longer distance ties.

Model III (Period 3, 4th-order proximal point)

It is challenging to create models that assume that particular communities engaged in long-distance travel, but if we assume that one feature of social life in the period after 2000 BP is that communities more commonly fostered ties with their nearest geographic neighbors, we can generate a so-called proximal point analysis (PPA) of the study region (Figure 4) (Broodbank 2000: 183 – 210; Terrell 1977: 34 – 39). A PPA model is constructed by choosing a certain number of neighbors (x) and linking each site to its (x) geographically nearest neighbors. In the present case, we chose a 4th-order PPA, as this is the minimal number of connections per node required to link all parts of the network into a single component. The more commonly utilized 3rd-order method in this particular case fails to link the Admiralty Islands and its obsidian sources to any other island groups, and therefore makes it impossible for Lou and Pam Island obsidians to reach areas where

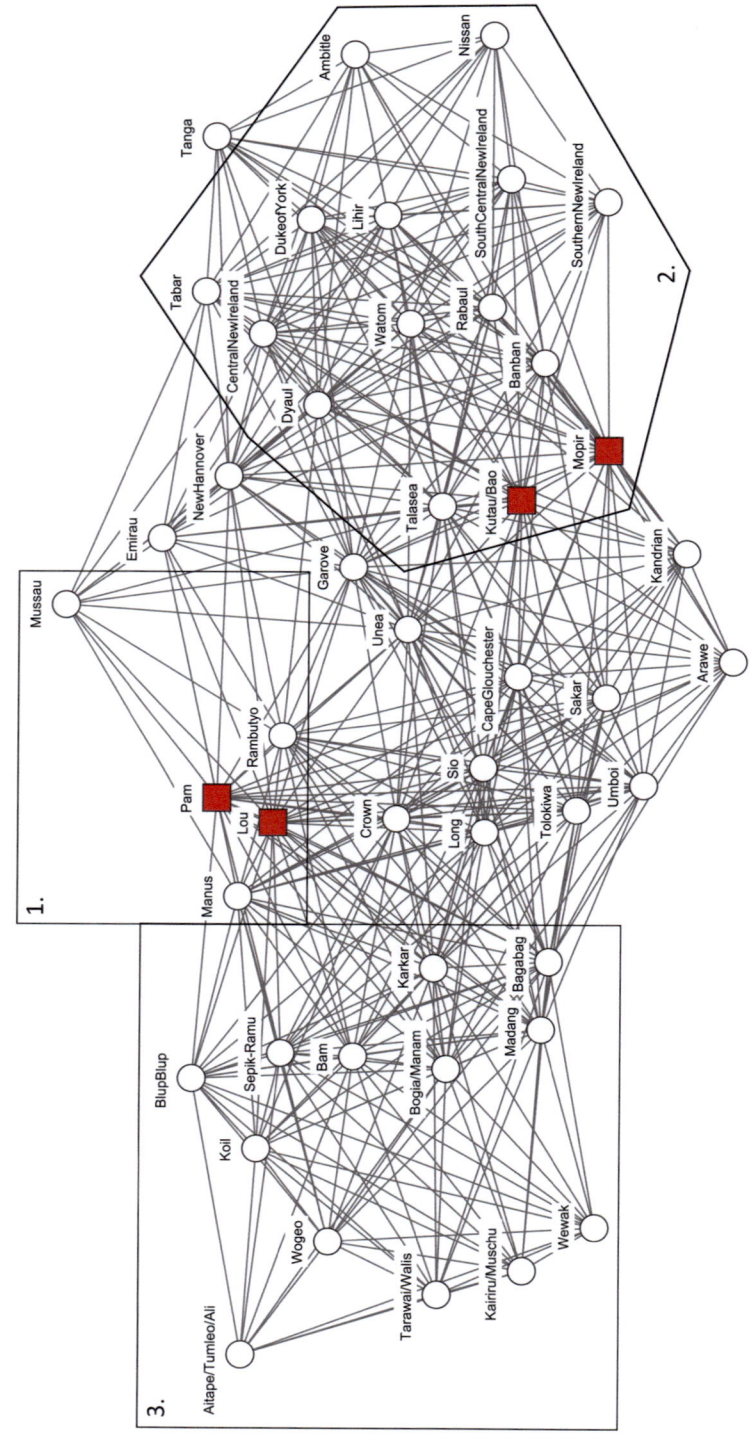

Figure 3: Voyaging model based on a maximal customary or possible distance of 360km. Areas are denoted where (1) Admiralty obsidian sources are more network proximal; (2) New Britain sources are more network proximal and should appear at higher frequency; and (3) both sources areas should be present, but Admiralty sources should predominate due to greater proximity. All other nodes are approximately equidistant between the two major source areas.

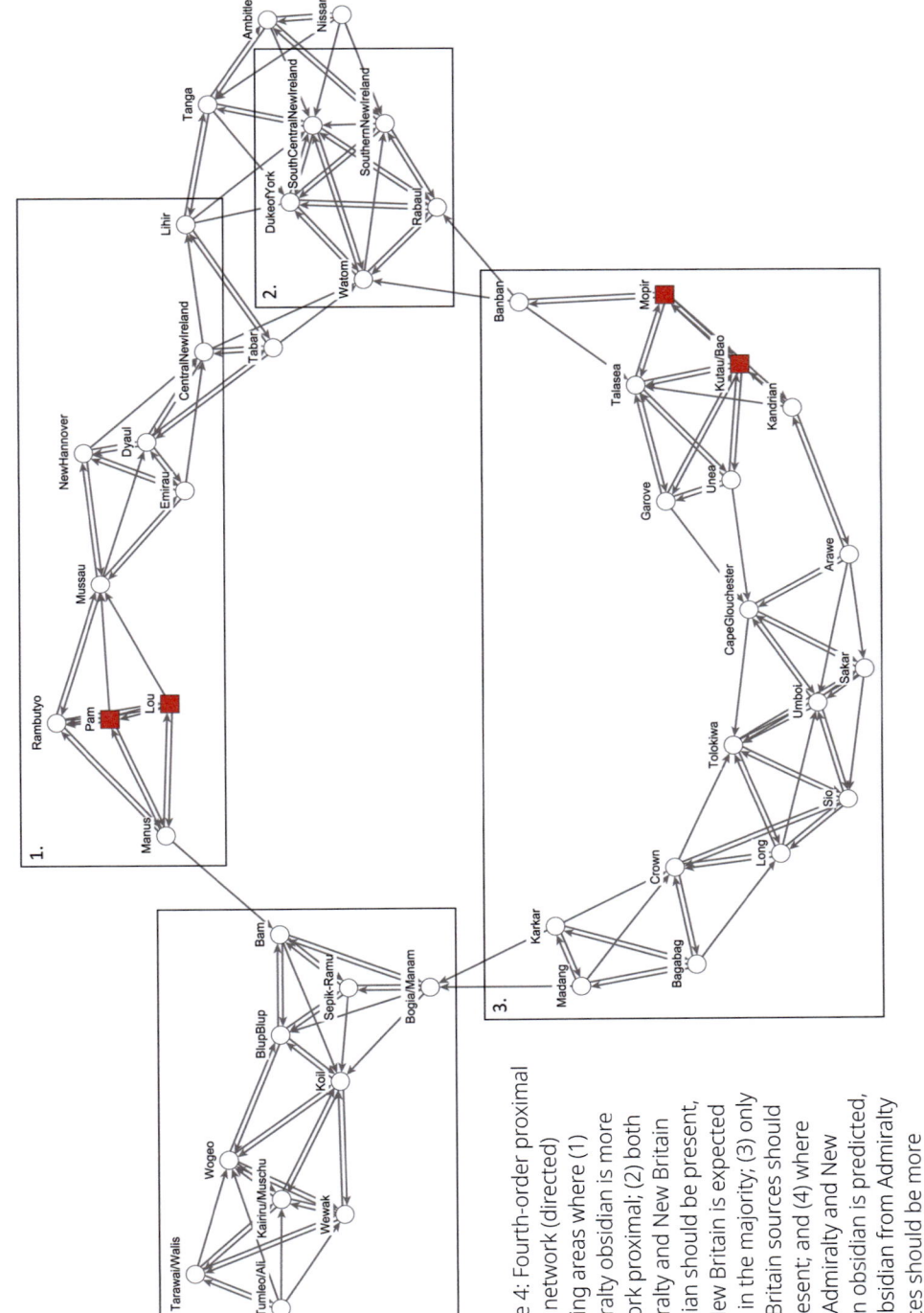

Figure 4: Fourth-order proximal point network (directed) showing areas where (1) Admiralty obsidian is more network proximal; (2) both Admiralty and New Britain obsidian should be present, but New Britain is expected to be in the majority; (3) only New Britain sources should be present; and (4) where both Admiralty and New Britain obsidian is predicted, but obsidian from Admiralty sources should be more frequent.

it is found in archaeological contexts dating to the post-2000 BP period. While Model III primarily consists of shorter distance ties, due to the presence of relatively geographically isolated nodes, some geographically longer-distance connections are retained, for instance the link between the Admiralty Islands and the north coast of mainland New Guinea evident on figure 4.

Assessing the models

To evaluate our models, we compiled a listing of all published obsidian assemblages sourced for the New Guinea region (see Figure 1 for locations and chronological assignments). While most obsidian sourcing studies in the Pacific have been carried out using chemical methods such as PIGME-PIXE, XRF, LA-ICP-MS, or INAA, a number of early studies utilized the relative density method, which is only capable of reliably distinguishing between the Admiralty Island and New Britain source areas and not between sub-sources within these two source regions (Torrence and Victor 1995: 130). Consequently, we pooled all data into these broad source region categories, and tabulated the relative contribution of Admiralty and New Britain material to each archaeological assemblage (by percentage of sourced artifacts) and only for assemblages from secure chronological contexts (either associated with radiometric dates or with well dated diagnostic ceramics).

There are interpretive challenges when applying network analysis to archaeological data. Borgatti and colleagues (Borgatti and Halgin 2011:1172, Borgatti and Lopez-Kidwell 2014: 40-41) argue that there are two metaphors commonly used to describe and interpret edges (ties) connecting network nodes – they may be viewed as girders that form the structural support for an overarching social topology, or they may be viewed as conduits through which social activity flows. Here, we adopt the flow model of ties, viewing them as potential pathways through which people, and the goods they transported, moved in prehistory. This does not imply that every pathway present in a model was utilized at all times, or even equally, only that people could have used any of the pathways present in a given model. Likewise, we assume a simple fall-off pattern for materials from their sources, such that network distance from source should impact how frequently represented a particular raw material source is, particularly when hundreds or thousands of years of prehistoric activity are pooled.

We present comparisons of shortest path lengths (the number of unweighted network steps) between each geographic node and each of the four obsidian source areas (Lou, Pam, Talasea/Willaumez Peninsula, and Mopir) in comparison to which obsidian source area is predominant at nearby archaeological sites (Table 1).

Model I

In the 220km threshold network model, three geographical/network regions with different patterns of obsidian availability should be present – in the first, comprising the Admiralty

Table 1 (opposite page): Locations included in the network models, network distances from each major source area in each model, and obsidian representation for geographically nearby assemblages during periods P1 (pre-3500 BP), P2 (3500-2000/1500 BP), and P3 (2000/1500 BP-present). T = Talasea/Willaumez Peninsula, M = Mopir, L = Lou Island, P = Pam Island. Network distances denoted as "nr" indicate sites that cannot be reached from a particular source area.

Node	220 km				Obsidian	360 km				Obsidian	4th-order PPA				Obsidian
	T	M	L	P	P1	T	M	L	P	P2	T	M	L	P	P3
Manus	5	5	1	1	A	2	2	1	1	A	12	11	1	1	A
Rambutyo	4	4	1	1	--	2	2	1	1	--	11	10	1	1	--
Mussau	3	3	2	2	--	2	2	1	1	A>NB	10	9	1	1	A>>NB
Emirau	3	3	3	3	--	2	1	1	1	A>>NB	9	8	2	2	--
New Hannover	3	3	3	3	--	1	1	1	1	--	9	8	2	2	--
Dyaul	2	2	3	3	--	1	1	2	2	--	8	7	2	2	--
Central New Ireland	2	2	4	4	NB	1	1	2	2	--	8	7	3	3	A>NB
Tabar	3	3	4	4	--	1	1	2	2	--	7	6	3	3	A
Lihir	3	3	4	4	NB	1	1	2	2	--	6	5	4	4	A
Tanga	3	3	5	5	--	2	2	2	2	--	5	4	5	5	A
Ambitle	3	3	5	5	--	2	2	3	3	NB≈A	5	4	6	6	A
Nissan	3	3	5	5	--	2	2	3	3	A≈NB	6	5	6	6	A>NB
South Central New Ireland	2	2	5	5	NB	1	1	2	2	--	4	3	6	6	NB>>A
Southern New Ireland	2	2	5	5	--	1	1	3	3	--	4	3	6	6	NB>>A
Duke of York	2	2	4	4	--	1	1	2	2	NB≈A	4	3	5	5	--
Watom	2	2	4	4	--	1	1	2	2	A≈NB	3	2	4	4	NB>>A
Rabaul	2	2	4	4	--	1	1	2	2	--	3	2	5	5	--
Banban	1	1	4	4	NB	1	1	2	2	--	2	1	nr	nr	--
Talasea	1	1	4	4	NB	1	1	2	2	NB	1	1	nr	nr	NB
Garove	1	1	5	5	--	1	1	1	1	--	1	1	nr	nr	--
Cape Glouchester	1	2	5	5	NB	1	1	1	1	--	2	3	nr	nr	--
Unea	1	1	5	5	--	1	1	1	1	--	1	2	nr	nr	--
Arawe	1	1	5	5	--	1	1	2	2	NB>>A	2	3	nr	nr	NB
Kandrian	1	1	5	5	NB	1	1	2	2	--	1	2	nr	nr	NB
Umboi	2	2	6	6	--	1	1	1	1	NB>>A	3	4	nr	nr	NB
Sakar	1	2	6	6	--	1	1	1	1	--	3	4	nr	nr	--
Tolokiwa	2	2	6	6	--	1	1	1	1	--	3	4	nr	nr	--
Sio	2	2	6	6	--	1	1	1	1	--	4	4	nr	nr	NB
Long	2	3	6	6	--	1	2	1	1	--	4	5	nr	nr	NB
Crown	2	3	6	6	--	1	2	1	1	--	4	5	nr	nr	--
Madang	3	3	7	7	NB	2	2	1	1	--	6	7	nr	nr	NB
Karkar	3	3	7	7	--	2	2	1	1	--	5	6	nr	nr	--
Bagabag	2	3	7	7	--	2	2	1	1	--	5	6	nr	nr	--
Bogia/Manam	3	4	8	8	--	2	2	1	1	--	6	7	3	3	--
Bam	3	4	8	8	--	2	2	1	1	--	7	8	2	2	--
Blup Blup	3	4	8	8	--	2	3	1	1	--	8	9	3	3	--
Sepik-Ramu	3	4	8	8	NB	3	3	1	1	--	7	8	3	3	--
Wewak	4	5	9	9	--	3	3	2	2	--	8	9	5	5	A>>NB
Koil	4	5	9	9	--	2	3	1	2	--	7	8	3	3	--
Wogeo	4	5	9	9	--	3	3	2	2	--	8	9	4	4	--
Kairiru/Muschu	4	5	9	9	--	3	3	2	2	--	8	9	4	4	A
Tarawai/Walis	4	5	9	9	--	3	3	2	2	--	10	11	6	6	A>>NB
Aitape/Tumleo/Ali	5	6	10	10	--	3	3	2	2	A>NB (?)	11	12	7	7	A>>NB

Islands themselves, Admiralty obsidian should predominate, while in the St. Matthias Group and on New Hannover, Admiralty obsidian should be more frequent than New Britain obsidian. In the remainder of the network, including all of New Ireland and its offshore islands, New Britain, and the New Guinea mainland and attendant island groups, New Britain obsidian should be more frequent. While we have a somewhat limited suite of data to assess this model, what is known of the distribution of obsidian stemmed tools prior to 3500 BP is in line with these modeling expectations – all stemmed tools recovered from New Britain and the mainland of New Guinea to date that have been sourced were made from obsidian from sources on New Britain, primarily the Kutau/Bao source in the Talasea/Willaumez Peninsula area. Tools of Admiralty obsidian have to date been found only on Manus and its surrounding islands, with the exception of a poorly provenienced stemmed tool found on Biak Island in West Papua, located outside of our study region (Torrence et al. 2009: 130).

Stemmed tools have not been found to date in the St. Matthias Group, where roughly equal amounts of obsidian from each source area are predicted by our model to have been present. However, the sharing of complex reduction strategies for stemmed tools, which are unlikely to have arisen independently, as well as the participation of Admiralty and St. Matthias Group islanders in shared mortar-and-pestle stylistic traditions during this time indicate that the circumscription of obsidian sources to particular regions was probably not due to complete isolation between the Admiralties and the rest of the SW Pacific, but rather because the structure and/or nature of inter-community ties inhibited the flow of Admiralty obsidian to New Ireland and beyond.

While there are insufficient empirical data available to determine how far Admiralty obsidian was transported during the mid-Holocene, we can compare network structure to stylistic patterning in the known distribution of mortars and pestles, assuming that more frequent interactions will increase the likelihood of producing and using similar forms of material culture. Applying the Girvan-Newman algorithm (Girvan and Newman 2002: 7822 – 7823) to the 220km threshold model indicates the existence of four likely network neighborhoods, comprising (1) the Admiralties and St. Matthias Group, (2) New Ireland/eastern New Britain, (3) western New Britain and the eastern Shouten Islands, and (4) the Sepik-Ramu and further westward. These network neighborhoods neatly align with the distribution of stylistic variants for mortars and pestles as currently understood (Torrence and Swadling 2008: fig. 5).

Model II

Model II is more densely connected than Model I with substantially shorter network distances between nodes and obsidian sources. The Model II network can be roughly divided into three regions, one in which the Admiralty sources are more network proximal than New Britain sources (comprising the Admiralty Islands and St. Matthias group as well as the north coast of mainland New Guinea between Aitape to the west and Bogia/Manam to the east), one in which the New Britain sources are more proximal (New Ireland and its offshore archipelagoes, and New Britain as far west as the Willaumez Peninsula source area), and an area in which the source areas are equidistant (New Britain west of the Willaumez Peninsula, the islands of the Vitiaz Straits, and the mainland and offshore islands as far west as Karkar).

In many parts of this study area, Model II provides a good fit to the observed distribution of obsidian frequencies, including the Admiralty Islands and St. Matthias Group, and the Vitiaz Straits area, where Admiralty Island obsidian appears at low frequencies on Tuam Island (near Umboi). These pieces are currently the only examples of Admiralty obsidian found in the Vitiaz Straits, which is geographically relatively close to the New Britain source areas – Admiralty obsidian is absent from assemblages dating to the post-Lapita period (Lilley 1986: 373 – 374). However, sites that are approximately network equidistant from the two obsidian source areas have an array of observed frequencies – sites located on and around New Britain like Watom, the Duke of Yorks, and the Arawe Islands, all of which are one step closer to New Britain sources than Admiralty sources, show a wide range of obsidian frequencies ranging from New Britain being far more common (Arawe Islands) to Admiralty sources being slightly more frequent (Watom). Unfortunately, there is no obsidian securely dated to Period 2 for the entire north coast of mainland New Guinea. Lapita sherds have been found with obsidian in the Aitape area, but only as surface collections – on Ali Island, obsidian recovered from a surface scatter that also contained a Lapita sherd consisted of 86% Admiralty obsidian and 14% New Britain obsidian (Golitko et al. 2013: 49), as would be roughly predicted by Model II. However, the association between pottery and obsidian on Ali is not secure.

Model III

Unlike the first two models, Model III is a directional network – one place can link to another without the link being reciprocated. We assume that obsidian primarily flows outward from sources along network ties. This assumption results in four network zones with different expectations for obsidian source representation. The Admiralty Islands, St. Matthias Group, northern areas of New Ireland, and its off-shore islands from Tabar to Nissan are more network proximal to the Admiralty sources than New Britain sources. Central and Southern New Ireland as well as the Duke of Yorks, Watom, and northern New Britain are closer to the New Britain sources but remain linked at a distance to the Admiralty sources. Only New Britain obsidian can reach the region between Banban Island and the Madang/Karkar area of the north coast in Model III, while the mainland north coast from Bogia/Manam westwards is closer to the Admiralty sources but can be reached from the New Britain obsidian sources.

Model III matches the observed distribution of obsidians in the post-2000 BP period closely (Table 1), with only New Britain obsidian found in the area unreachable by Admiralty obsidian (area 3 on Figure 4), stretching as far west as Bogia/Manam, Admiralty obsidian far more frequent on the north coast west of that point, and Admiralty obsidian much more frequent in network region 1 (Figure 4). In particular, the division of New Ireland into two procurement areas – which matches observed frequencies – cannot be generated using only a distance threshold, but emerges from assuming predominantly proximal interactions in our node set. The only major deviance from model expectations in this case concerns Tabar, Lihir, and Tanga, which are approximately equidistant from the two source areas, but where excavated assemblages contain only Admiralty obsidian. Nissan, slightly further to the south, has obsidians from both source areas, as predicted by model III.

Here, the limitations of using straight-line distances in cases where edges cross islands rather than predominantly following ocean routes is evident. If overland routes that cross

New Ireland (Tabar to Watom, and Tanga and Lihir to the Duke of Yorks) are removed, the model prediction better matches archaeological observation as well as ethnographically documented patterns of trade in the region which linked these islands to the northern coast of New Ireland but not beyond (Terrell 1986:140), suggesting that in these cases (Kandrian and Arawe may be also be impacted), Model III does not adequately account for the friction of overland movement relative to marine transport.

For areas in which modelled connections do not include overland transport (e.g., where straight-line distances are entirely across water), Model III otherwise compares well to the ethnographic record. For instance, the trade between the Admiralties and mainland north coast was carried out by Manus sailors, who voyaged between the Admiralty sources on Lou and Pam and the Shouten Islands of Bam, Koil, and Wogeo via the uninhabited Purdy Islands (Amborse1976:358, 1978: 329; Hogbin 1935: 396 – 397). Materials were further distributed along the north coast by islander middlemen (Koil, Tarawai, Ali) as well as the residents of the Murik Lakes region (Sepik-Ramu delta) (Lipset 1985: 81 – 83). Further east, Siassi traders (Umboi and surrounding islands) moved Talasea obsidian, pottery, and other goods through a network that spanned the western portions of New Britain, the islands of the Vitiaz straits, and the mainland coast between Sio and Madang (Harding 1967: 9 – 19).

Discussion

These models highlight how a few relatively basic structural considerations applied to geographic distances can generate models in line with archaeological observations without requiring us to consider major transformations to the majority of the network ties connecting communities to one another in the past. Within a radius of 20-50 km – a distance between communities that might be traversed quite regularly within one or two days of walking, paddling, or sailing – the three models are effectively identical to one another. By altering only the structure of longer-distance (and likely less frequently utilized) social ties in our models, major changes in obsidian distribution can be reproduced. Consequently, our analysis shows that the changing distribution of obsidian around the Bismarck Sea during most of the Holocene period can be explained without having to alter much about the everyday lived experience of the people resident there or the everyday social contacts they maintained.

Given this result, we question how much can be read into the varying distribution of obsidian over time as it pertains to the identity of those embedded in the prehistoric networks through which volcanic glass was transported. While Lapita was once viewed as a cohesive package of new material innovations transported into the Pacific from somewhere in Island Southeast Asia (ISEA), nowadays few archaeologists working in the region would argue for the simultaneous introduction of all features of what has been called the "Lapita Cultural Complex" into the Bismarck Sea region (Specht et al. 2014: 119). It is now evident that technological innovations such as shell working (Szabó and O'Connor 2004: 625 – 626), stone adze production (Specht et al. 2014: 105 – 106), and pottery making (Gaffney et al. 2015 : 12) as well as flora (banana, taro, breadfruit) and fauna (pigs, chickens, and dogs) (Specht 2010: 108 – 116), genes (Soares et al. 2011: 242), and probably language practices (Donohue and Denham 2010: 229) all moved back and forth between the southwestern Pacific and ISEA beginning minimally during the early Holocene. Yet most models of this process remain wedded to a dichotomy between mass migration of

Austronesian speakers and adoption of new traits by people long resident in the region (Specht et al. 2014: 92 – 93).

More than half a century of network research shows that social networks approximate a so-called "small-world," characterized both by strong tie-based clustering and by weaker ties between these cliques that produce short average paths between any two individuals or places (Schnettler 2009: 166 – 167). Consequently, information, ideas, innovations, and so forth can move relatively easily between network cliques unless these cliques are extremely closed (e.g., some religious cults). While our models are simple, they do show that it is possible to generate observed patterns of obsidian distribution in the circum-Bismarck Sea region without radically changing the structure of local interactions, and that it may be necessary to model the region as a single connected network component in order to do so.

Notably, networks are highly dynamic – weak ties may transform into strong ties, adopting new shared practices may generate a sense of association where none previously existed ("homophily by social influence" in network parlance), and the structure, geographic distribution, and membership of cliques can shift over time both through social influence and through actual movement of people along the geographical ties that link communities and places to one another. Our models suggest that the supposedly major transformations in interaction networks that occurred after 3500 BP could have resulted from something as simple as the introduction of new voyaging technology, and that expansion of obsidian distribution at this time may map these voyages. Whether these canoes were associated with the speaker of one language or another may consequently be more difficult to derive from the distribution of raw material than some would suppose. Lapita pottery may have been but one new technological and cultural innovation among many that entered the region between about 6000 and 3000 BP, as Torrence and Swadling have previously suggested (Torrence and Swadling 2008: 613 – 614). We suggest that the distribution and use of Lapita ceramics could be viewed as part of an emergent community of practice that was qualitatively little different from the earlier shared practice of making and decorating stone mortars and pestles and knapping large obsidian stemmed tools during the preceding mid-Holocene period (Terrell 2014: 9 – 10), or the world of island middlemen, interlinked "trade spheres," and regionalized ceramic styles that followed. More generally, we suggest that archaeologists should focus more on generating plausible models of social structure and dynamics based on both the real world constraints of geography, as well as the insights offered by social network approaches.

Conclusions

Using only geographical distances and a set of simple assumptions about changes to the structure of longer distance connections, we are able to model and reproduce known changes in the distribution of obsidian from source areas on New Britain and in the Admiralty Islands for the period between 6000 BP and the present. Our models retain essentially the same geographically local structure of ties, and at least for the transition between the mid-Holocene and the later Holocene, only require us to assume that people resident in some communities in the region obtained the skills and know-how to produce and use outrigger canoes with sails to cross longer distances than had previously been possible. Whether these models hold up to further scrutiny remains to be seen, but they have the advantage of being predictive relative to areas in which obsidian has to date either not been found, or has been found but not sourced, and can consequently be tested with future field and laboratory investigation.

Networks provide a set of tools with which archaeologists can formally examine and test their assumptions and models of the past. We would argue that a network perspective is basically different from the conventional archaeological view of the past, predicated on bounded social groups that remain coherent both in space and time. The network approach allows us to move beyond simple dichotomies between isolation and contact to examine how differential abilities and motivations to seek particular social connections generate patterning in the archaeological record. Paying more attention both to what we know of the structure of human social networks, the motivations for establishing social connections both near and far, and how network structure and activity pattern the archaeological record may help archaeologists move beyond dichotomies between migration and stasis predicated on a categorical view of human biocultural diversity.

Acknowledgements

We would like to thank Helen Dawson and Francesco Iacono for inviting us to Berlin to participate in "Bridging Geographical and Social Space through Networks" and the Topoi Excellence Cluster for funding our participation.

Terrestrial Transportation Networks and Power Balance in Etruria and Latium Vetus between the beginning of the Early Iron Age and the end of the Archaic Period

Francesca Fulminante, Alessandro Guidi, Sergi Lozano, Ignacio Morer, Luce Prignano

Terrestrial transportation networks, modelling, central Italy, Iron Age urbanisation

Introduction

In the last ten years, increasing attention has been devoted to understanding settlement systems through the application of Central Place Theory, locational models, Proximal Point Analysis, as well as gravitation and other interaction models (see for example, Fulminante 2014 with reference to previous studies, or more recently Nakoinz 2013a, b, c, Bevan and Wilson 2013, Paliou and Bevan 2016, Evans et al. 2013, Evans and Rivers 2017, Palmisano 2017). Such studies usually focus on the relative importance of the sites and attempt to work out to what extent general factors (*e.g.*, topography or social-ecological advantages) can explain why some places become more prominent than others. The data they take as input are largely limited to size and position of settlements, frequently the most homogeneous data available to archaeologists.[1]

The issue of whether and how settlements located in a certain territory were organised at the regional level is considerably more difficult and can be regarded as mostly unresolved. Whilst the existence of a certain degree of regional organisation can be tackled by techniques for the analysis of site distributions such as nearest-neighbour

---

[1] Today new approaches are also trying to include cultural factors in network approaches by using different types of material culture, which is partially more complex given the heterogeneity and fragmentary nature of archaeological research and data, but seems very promising (see *e.g.* Fulminante forthcoming and contributions in Donnelan 2020); and more specifically attempting to combine Central Place Theory with Network Analysis such as in the innovative approach by Nakoinz et al. 2020 with previous references.

analysis (Pinder et al. 1979), that help distinguishing between randomly distributed and clustered (organized) settlements, more complex matters remain out of reach. To what extent did past communities cooperate or compete? Were they just struggling for their individual benefit or were they aware of their interdependence? These are just a few questions that can in principle be addressed quantitatively, but what kind of data is suitable for hypothesis selection when dealing with these issues?

In a recent work (Prignano et al. 2019), we propose to gain a better understanding about these important topics by analysing Terrestrial Transportation Infrastructures (TTI). Indeed, the system of roads that existed in a territory might encode the footprint of processes and interactions at the regional scale. Starting from the Bronze Age, but even more with the advent of the Iron Age, the increasing social complexity and the accumulation of resources set the conditions for humans to have both the incentive and the capability to build roads (Lay 1992, Earle 2011(1991)). Constructed roads flourished along with the development of urban societies, when performing cuts, building bridges, or removing obstacles became both necessary and affordable.

The importance of TTI for the understanding of the political and social organisation of the communities that created and maintained them has been previously assessed, for example in relation to the Roman Empire (*e.g.*, Chevallier 1976, Taylor 1979, Crumley and Marquadt 1987, Purcell 1990, Mattingly 1997. In the 1990's Trombold presented an important collection of works on TTI in the New World (Trombold 2011 (1991), followed by Jenkins 2001 and Smith 2005). Recently, a renewed interest in TTI seems to have produced a number of new studies in Pre-Roman and Roman Europe (*e.g.*, Nakoinz 2012a, b; Faupel 2018; Faupel and Nakoinz 2018; Filet 2017; Groenhuijzen and Verhagen 2016; Verhagen et al. 2019), suggesting that this is a growing field of research (see *e.g.* recent projects such as ORBIS[2] by Stanford University, or the New Transhumance project in Toscana, Pizziolo et al. 2016).

Building on this literature, we propose to take a further step and try to infer aspects of the political organisation of a region from the quantitative analysis of TTI. In particular, we will focus on roads that connected human communities with each other, since their function was directly related with inter-settlement interactions (between villages, towns, and cities), and it is hence sensible to assume that they were the output of a collective effort for the benefit of one or more of the parties involved. More specifically, we developed a baseline methodology to contrast hypotheses about the organisation of a system of settlements, starting from a regional road map. Such a methodology consists of three fundamental ingredients: 1) a procedure for extracting relevant quantitative data from road maps; 2) a set of competing hypotheses about organisational aspects of road construction; and 3) formal models translating such hypotheses into mechanisms for generating synthetic data to be compared against the empirical ones. The underlying idea is that some models reproduce relevant features of the empirical TTI with higher accuracy than others. Thus, we can determine which hypothesis (or hypotheses) better explains the empirical evidence and is therefore more likely to resemble the actual mechanisms of organisation. To develop such a methodology, we adopted network science as a general framework. We regard this as a natural choice, given that we chose to focus on road networks because of the information embedded in their connectivity and functionality.

---

2   See http://orbis.stanford.edu/orbis2012.

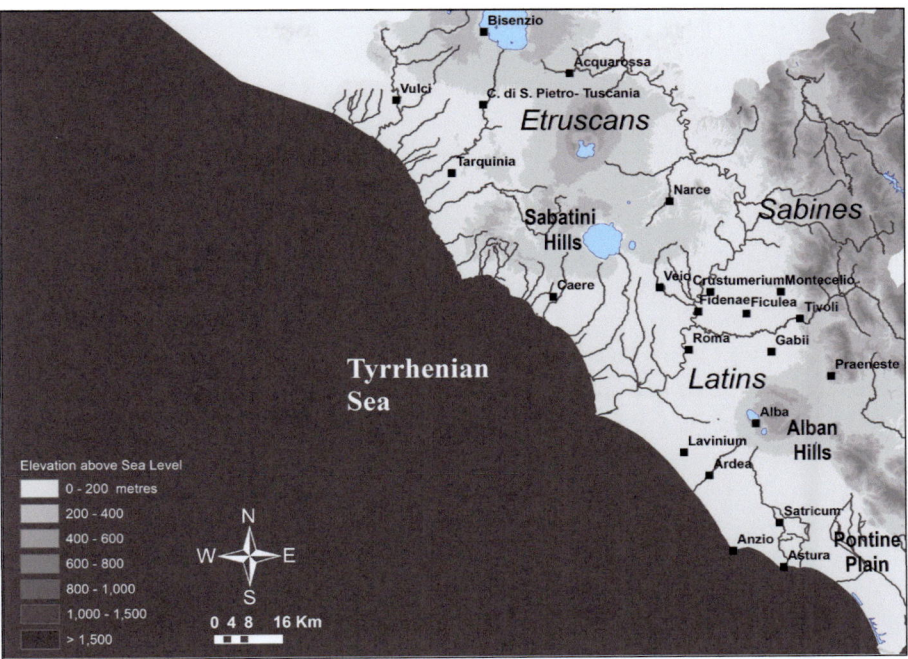

Figure 1: Southern Etruria and Latium vetus in Central Italy.

Network science provides us both an analytical toolbox for the characterisation of such aspects of TTI and a conceptual framework for model building (Prignano et al. 2019).

Here, we summarise and compare the results obtained for two different but related case studies: Iron Age Southern Etruria, a paradigmatic case we used for testing our technique (Prignano et al. 2019), and coeval neighbouring Latium vetus (Fulminante et al. 2017) (Figure 1). Both Southern Etruria and Latium vetus are very well-studied contexts, with detailed archaeological information about settlement patterns and an established tradition of studies on TTI. Obviously TTI are more archaeologically visible in later phases, during the Roman Era and partially in the Etruscan period, when road cuts and stone build roads start to appear. However, as we will show in the methodology section, Iron Age and Orientalising period routes have also been reconstructed (and traced on maps) based on direct (settlements position and alignments) and indirect evidence (existence of later roads on the same route). There is a wide degree of consensus among scholars on the trajectory especially of main routes connecting primary larger settlements.

Between the beginning of the Iron Age and the Archaic Period, (southern) Etruria underwent a complex process of urbanisation (see *e.g.* Stoddart and Spivey 1990, Barker and Rasmussen 1998, Rasmussen 2005, Bonghi Jovino 2005, Pacciarelli 2001, 2010, 2017, Riva 2010, Marino 2015, Stoddart 2016, Stoddart 2020). It was dominated by a number of equally ranked proto-urban centres that went on to develop into the city-states of the Orientalising and Archaic Period (Veii, Tarquinia, Caere, Vulci, Orvieto, and now also Bisenzio) characterised by a strong common identity but also by distinctive local "flavours" (Bietti Sestieri 2010). None of these centres were able to prevail over the others and impose on them a guiding role (Guidi 1985). Therefore, it has been suggested that at this time Etruria was characterised by an overall balanced dynamics of power (Fulminante and Stoddart 2012 and Stoddart et al. 2020).

Latium vetus was also organised in proto-urban centres and later city-states with a common material culture (Latial culture I-IV), similar burial costumes and a similar socio-political organisation (see *e.g.* Smith 1996, Smith 2007, Carafa 2014, Fulminante 2014, 2018 and Mogetta 2014). These polities were characterised by cooperative/competitive behaviours according to the model of the peer-polity interactions (Renfrew 1986, Verhagen 2015). However, in this region the power was quite unbalanced. In particular, it seems undeniable that around 950/900 BC, with the shift of the funerary areas from the Forum to the Esquiline and Quirinal Hill, Rome became by far the largest settlement in the region and lately emerged as a centralised authority with a noticeable disruption in the balance between the city-states (already Guidi 1982 and more recently Carandini 1997, Alessandri 2007, 2013 and Fulminante 2014).

In this paper, we compare the TTI of the two regions, Etruria and Latium vetus, in order to highlight similarities and differences that characterise these two different complex systems, and better understand how the two systems actually worked and whether similarities or differences in the TTI reflect different socio-political systems or at least different balance of power and interaction patterns within similar socio-political systems.

Methodology

Our purpose is to infer how settlements were organised at the regional level by analysing the structure formed by the roads that connected them. The basic idea is to compare different hypotheses and quantitatively assess which of them is (or are) more plausible and, as stated above, we do this in three steps. Adopting a network science approach implies that the first step we have to take is to translate available information on pathways from the usual map format into networks, *i.e.*, mathematical structures made up of interconnected objects. Once the empirical system is mapped onto weighted geographical networks, one can apply the established analytic tools provided by network science for their characterisation.

However, such a methodology cannot consist of a mere analysis of network properties: we need to link the observed properties to the mechanisms that generated them. The final output of the application of the proposed technique consists of statements of the type "since we made an observation X, then process Y is more likely to have occurred than process Z". Therefore, as a second step, we had to hypothesise generative mechanisms that might have created the empirical network and to contrast their different outcomes (synthetic networks) against the empirical evidence. More concretely, we devised competing network models, each one corresponding to a strategy according to which the nodes made decisions about which links had to be established.

The third and last step is the validation of the proposed models. We tested whether the synthetic networks that they generated were able of reproducing structural features of the empirical networks with satisfactory accuracy. If there existed at least one among them whose output resembled closely enough the empirical observations, then we could conclude that its underlying mechanism shared some similarities with the actual processes that generated the TTI under study. In the following subsections, we describe in more details each one of the methodological steps.

Construction of the empirical networks

For this study, we considered all known Southern Etruria and Latium vetus settlements between the beginning of the Early Iron Age and the end of the Archaic Period that are larger than 1 ha. A dataset of Latium vetus settlements had already been collected and analysed in another work by one of the authors (Fulminante 2014). The useful works on the same region by Luca Alessandri have also been consulted (Alessandri 2013, 2016). For Southern Etruria, our main references were the *Repertorio dei Siti Preistorici e Protostorici della Regione Lazio* (Belardelli *et al.* 2007), the *Dictionary of the Etruscans* (Stoddart 2009) and the work by Marco Rendeli on the territorial organization of Southern Etruria in the Orientalising and Archaic Period (Rendeli 1993). In addition, the list of settlements was updated on the basis of more recent publications in *Studi Etruschi*, and the most important conference proceedings (*e.g. Preistoria e Protostoria in Etruria, gli Annali della Fondazione per il Museo "C. Faina"*), as well as exhibition catalogues (*e.g.* Della Fina and Pellegrini 2013).

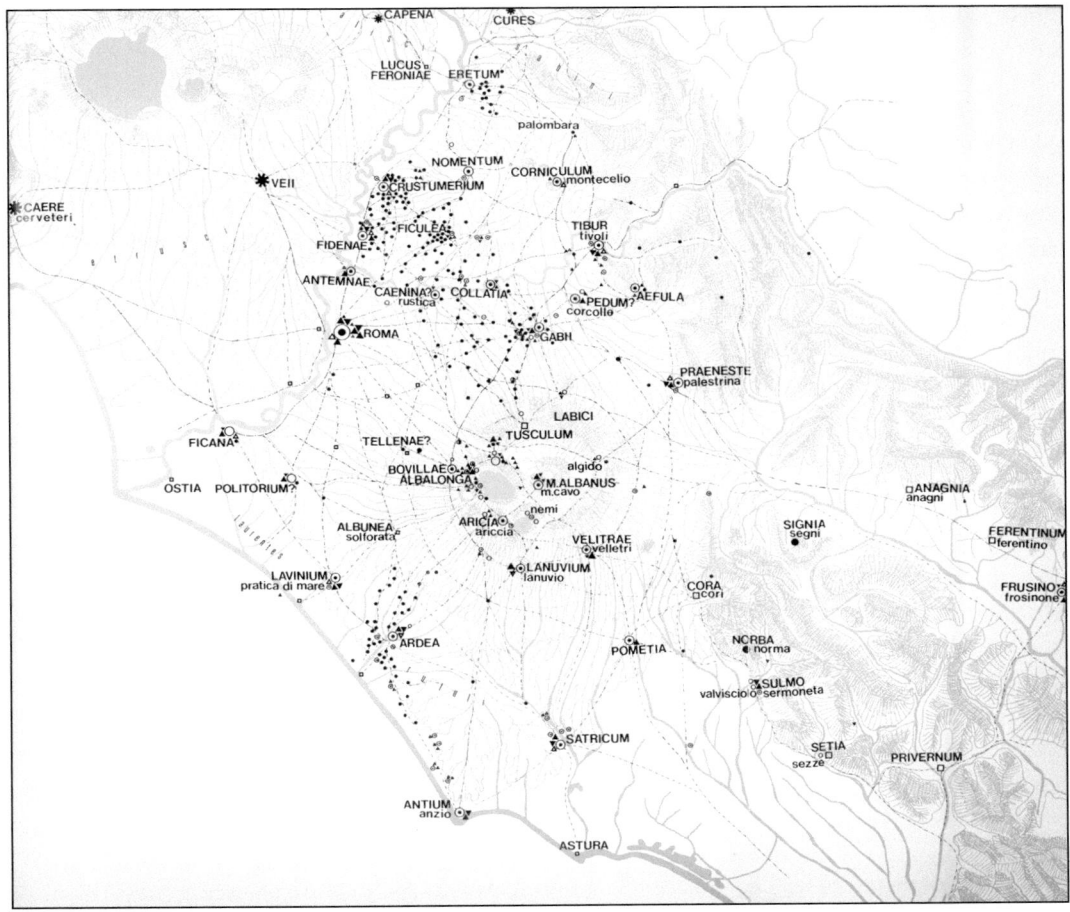

Figure 2: Latium Vetus terrestrial communication and transportation routes during the Archaic Period according to Lorenzo and Stefania Quilici Gigli (from Colonna 1976).

As mentioned in the introduction, prehistoric and proto-historic routes are less visible archaeologically because of their characteristics, being mainly track and used routes rather than monumental stone constructions. However, in the Italian archaeological and topographic tradition many scholars have tried to reconstruct these routes on the basis of the following principles: 1) topography of the region, 2) the position of settlements (and/or sanctuaries and funerary monuments) attested archaeologically (direct evidence) and 3) the remains of monumental roads of the later periods (inference on the base of later evidence). Therefore, there is a relatively established tradition of study which has reached a good consensus among scholars. For Latium vetus we used the reconstruction by Lorenzo and Stefania Quilici Gigli (in Colonna 1976) elaborated in a map at the regional level for the Archaic Period (Figure 2).

For the Etruscan region, unfortunately, a comprehensive study is still missing (but see Tuppi 2014). Therefore, we considered several works, whose authors also suggested reconstructed routes on maps (Potter 1979, 1985, Zifferero 1995, Tartara 1999, Brocato 2000, Enei 2001, Bonghi Jovino 2008, Schiappelli 2008). To test these suggested routes, we verified their alignment with settlements discovered more recently, after the publication of those works, and observed that they were generally coherent with those routes, so we are confident of the reliability of those reconstructions.

The task of translating road maps into networks is not straightforward and can be performed in many alternative, not equivalent ways. Since we are studying inter-settlement interactions, we need our nodes to be human communities with a certain degree of political agency, such that they could play an active role in shaping the regional infrastructure. Then, the simplest option for defining edges is to consider that a bidirectional link between two sites is established whenever they are directly connected by a terrestrial route, with no other settlement in between. Once the rules are set, the second stage consists in selecting and organising the empirical data.

By considering the maximum period in which the settlements co-existed without major changes, we obtained five time slices:

- Early Iron Age 1 Early (EIA1E): (950/925- 900 BC)
- Early Iron Age 1 Late (EIA1L): (900- 850/825 BC)
- Early Iron Age 2 (EIA2): (850/825- 730/720 BC)
- Orientalising Age (OA): (730/720- 580 BC)
- Archaic Period (AA): (580-500 BC)

Both settlements and communication routes have been considered as unchanging within each time slice. In this sense, the analysis considered five static networks rather than a system in evolution. Finally, since we were interested in terrestrial routes as the product of a collective effort, requiring the allocation of resources to be built and maintained, it was essential to somehow quantify their cost. It is reasonable to assume that, beyond the peculiarities of road building in each individual case, the cost of a road is roughly proportional to its length. To determine the length associated with each connection, we could have implemented GIS based analysis, measuring it directly in the case of known ways and adopting a least-cost path (LCP) approach for those paths whose route is not completely known. However, using such different levels of precision for different links might be detrimental. We concluded that the optimal way to address the geographical factor was to represent sites as geo-localised nodes and assign weights to the links according to the geodesic distance between the nodes they connect. This is a quite good approximation provided that the region is limited and presents a relatively homogeneous landscape, but more importantly, the lack of precision is evenly distributed among the nodes, without biases towards less studied areas (for a more exhaustive discussion of the benefits and issues of the available alternatives, see Prignano et al. 2019, Sec. 3.1).

As a final note, we have to acknowledge that we did not take into consideration either connections with settlements that do not belong to the regions under study or those that joined places on the two sides of the limit between the Latium vetus end Etruria. Since we analysed interactions between polities within the same regional system, and our focus is on the global scale, not on the properties of individual settlements, this is not a central issue for the present work. Nonetheless, we are aware that disregarding such links may affect some aspects of our results and we are currently investigating the importance of inter-regional connections in a new study that looks at the two regions as interdependent systems.

Characterisation of terrestrial route networks

We are interested in characterising TTIs by means of particular features that conditioned the way they functioned and determined their performance, i.e., the efficiency and robustness of the communication that took place on it. Such systemic features are not defined by individual connections between specific pairs of settlements but by all of them. For instance, we might focus overly on the presence of a few central places that are much better connected than many peripheral ones (inequality) or on the existence of routes or settlements that, if inaccessible, made the network fall apart (fragility). Hence, we selected and calculated five network metrics that translate in quantitative terms some relevant features of the TTI of Etruria and Latium vetus from the beginning of the Early Iron Age to the end of the Archaic Period. In other words, these indicators were chosen in such a way that two networks with similar values in all their measures are expected to perform similarly in terms of transportations and communication processes (Albert and Barabási 2002, Boccaletti et al. 2006).

The selected network measures are: 1) average node strength (also known as average weighted degree) $<s_i>$; 2) average edge length $<l>$; 3) average clustering coefficient $<C>$; 4) global efficiency $<E_{glob}>$; 5) local efficiency $<E_{loc}>$. These measures are explained in detail in a recent publication by the authors (Prignano et al. 2019). The first three measures are very common in network analysis and represent respectively: the mean total length of the links adjacent to a node; the mean of the weights (length) of all links present in the system; the presence of closed triangles in the network. The last two, however, are less common and specific of geographical network analysis.

In particular, the concept of efficiency can be applied to networks both at the local and global scale. The efficiency of communication between two sites is defined by the length of the shortest path (on the network) between them divided by the linear distance between their location: the longer the path between two nodes in comparison with their distance, the less efficient the network. The global efficiency is calculated as an average on all pairs of nodes.

The local efficiency measures the capacity of the network to react to a crisis at the local level. More concretely, the local efficiency of a node defines how efficiently information is shared and moved among neighbours if that node is eliminated. The overal value is obtained by averaging over all the nodes (Vragović et al. 2005).

Principles of network modelling

In order to gain a better understanding of how settlements were organised at the regional level, we analyse the structures formed by the roads that connected them searching for the mechanisms underlying the decision-making processes that created them. To this aim, we produced models able to generate "synthetic networks" from different hypothetical mechanisms and compared such networks with their empirical counterparts obtained as explained above, for each age and region.

The idea of network models as a means for explaining some features of real networked systems dates back to the late 1990s and builds up on a long tradition developed in the framework of mathematical sociology during the previous decades. Initially, the three most studied properties of social networks – and later on of other types of systems, such as citation networks, airport networks, or the world wide web, among many others – were the degree distribution (how many nodes have how many links), the clustering coefficient, and the average path length (the average number of steps along the shortest paths for all possible pairs of network nodes). A large part of empirical networks have heterogeneous degree distribution, high clustering coefficient, and very short path length (resulting in the famous "six degrees of separation"). Already in the 1970s, it was clear that this combination of features can neither be explained as the mere effect of chance nor can it be obtained by building connections according to simple mathematical rules. For instance, if we connect node pairs at random with a certain probability, by tuning such probability, we are able to reproduce the observed number of links of any empirical system, and the average path length is also likely to be close to the observed one. On the other hand, the degree distribution will be much more homogeneous and the clustering coefficient (related with number of triangles) significantly lower. Alternatively, it is straightforward to come up with a mathematical rule for connecting nodes such that the clustering coefficient is similar to the observed one, but then the average path length will be too large and the degree distribution still too homogeneous. Both random and regular networks reproduce some of the features of real networks, but they cannot display them altogether. This is the main motivation for the onset of network science: to answer the question of which mechanisms are able to generate the properties of real networks.[3]

Such mechanisms are implemented as algorithms that work in different fashions: in some cases, they take as a starting point a regular or random network and proceed to modify it by rewiring or adding connections; in some other cases, nodes are also added at each step. One of the most paradigmatic network models is the Barabási-Albert (BA) model (Albert and Barabási 2002), an algorithm that adds nodes one at a time. Each new node establishes a connection with any of the existing ones with a probability proportional to the links that the latter already has. In other words, the new nodes have a "preference" to attach themselves to the already heavily linked nodes. Thus, heavily linked nodes ("hubs") tend to quickly accumulate even more links, while those with only a few links are unlikely to be chosen as the destination for a new link. The BA algorithm simulates a system that experiences the well-known "the rich get richer" effect, and the resulting synthetic networks display a highly heterogeneous degree distribution. In more concrete terms, we

---

3   It is usual for network scientists to refer to the networks built on the bases of empirical observations as "real networks" to differentiate them from "artificial" or "model generated" graphs. However, in the context of archaeological studies, we preferred the term "empirical networks".

can imagine that each node is, for instance, a scholarly paper, while the links stand for citations. Although the actual criteria for selecting references are far more complicated than the mechanism implemented by the model – no one picks papers at random according to a certain probability – the BA algorithm captures a general trend (highly cited papers are more likely to be cited even more) and is able to reproduce a distinctive feature of real citation networks. In this way, the hypothesis that authors when building a list of references for a new publication tend to have a preference towards already popular papers, can be corroborated (even though it is not definitively proven, since it is still possible that another model implementing a different mechanism reproduces the same trait). Citation networks are not the only type of system that can be (partially) explained by the BA algorithm, which was originally devised as a network model for the Web. Its importance does not lie in its ability to perfectly reproduce some phenomena, but in the capability of capturing something general that is common to a wide range of systems. The same algorithm can be interpreted in many ways according to different contexts (nodes may be papers, websites, airports, hence links are citation, hyperlinks, flights, etc.), while the underlying mechanism stays unchanged. This is, roughly speaking, how network modelling works: an abstract mechanism (*e.g.*, the rich get richer) is translated into a generative algorithm for networks (*e.g.*, preferential attachment), but in order for the model to explain something specific of the system under study, we need an interpretative metaphor (*e.g.*, highly cited papers have greater visibility).

Network models for TTIs

In our work, each network model implements an algorithm that, starting from a certain number of disconnected sites (the settlements of the empirical networks), decides what links should be added to build up the artificial networks. The approach is similar to the BA model, but in this case the nodes are not characterised by the "timestamp" of their creation but rather by their geographical coordinates. They all exist in the initial state, while the links are created one at a time.

Since our goal was to unveil the basic principles governing the interaction between the different communities of a regional system, we had to consider a limited number of radically dissimilar scenarios. In the first one, settlements did not have information about the TTI at the regional scale, neither did they share any common interest; in the second one, they did have information at the regional scale, but shared no common interest; in the third and last one, they had both regional scale information and common interests. In all these cases, we made the general assumption that any settlement needed to be well connected, that is, they all actively tried to get as many links as possible. More specifically, we assumed that each settlement pursued being able to reach any other through a path as short as possible. The difference between the three scenarios lies in their means and criteria for setting priorities.

Once the basic assumptions were set, we proceeded to translate them into algorithms for establishing links between nodes. This step implies a certain degree of lack of determination since it can be performed in multiple ways. Simplicity was the guiding principle that shaped our models. Refinements are always possible afterwards, but the baseline needs to be directly connected with the main concept one wants to test, otherwise the interpretation of the result becomes more difficult and potentially ambiguous. Hence, we designed a minimalistic set up in which each node, at each step, had a preference about which link had to be built, and it was always a link connecting itself to another node which it considered to be the most beneficial for its connectivity. Such individual (local) preferences were sorted in different ways, depending on whether the settlements were interested in building a functional TTI at the regional scale (third scenario) or not (first and second scenarios). If they were interested only in their own connectivity, every settlement tried to establish its preferred link as the next step; otherwise, it tried to reach some kind of agreement with its neighbours and their individual preferences were sorted out according to a shared criterion. At the same time, the way they set their preferences depends on the information available to them.

After defining the abstract principles, we needed to translate them in terms of rules for establishing links, thus devising a set of generative network models.

For the sake of simplicity, we made the additional assumption that all node-settlements were intrinsically equally important. In other words, we did not make any supposition about their power, richness or attractiveness: our models take as an input no other node attribute beside the geographical position. In this way, the node-settlements based their choice on geographical (distances) and topological (already existing links) information only. In the first scenario, their knowledge was limited to the links that connected them to other nodes, while in the second and third ones, nodes knew any existing path joining them to any other place independently on the number of steps (intermediate nodes). Hence, in the first case, at each step, each node's preference was to build a new link with the closest node that was not already connected to it. On the contrary, in the case they had complete topological information (second and third scenarios), since their goal was to improve their connectivity, they would have preferred to compare the length of any existing path connecting them to any other node with the length of the corresponding direct link, to better assess the benefit of building it. In quantitative terms, the most beneficial link would be the one that minimises the ratio of its length to the length of the shortest existing path to the same node (best "shortcut").

Finally, we implemented the interplay between the individual node-settlement interests. If it was pure competition, then at each step every node tried to prevail over the rest and build its preferred link. A realistic simulation of such processes, besides being extremely difficult, would have not fit in with the minimalistic approach of network modelling. More importantly, it was not necessary. We took a step back and assumed that the output of the competitive interactions between node-settlements was indeterminate. Each node had the chance to prevail at each step, according to a certain probability distribution, but we did not know a priori which one was going to build a new link at the next step. Therefore, the corresponding network models (first and second scenarios) were not deterministic. If we ran them several times, they generated several different networks -similarly to what happens with the BA model- and their outputs had to be analysed statistically. To avoid making arbitrary assumptions, at this stage, we decided that the probability distribution had to be uniform, that is, each node had the same chance to prevail at each step.

The third scenario presents a radically different situation. Since in this case the nodes were supposed to reach an agreement and decide collectively which link had to be built at each step, we had to set a criterion for doing so. The settlements would have compared their individual preferences and settled for the most beneficial at the regional scale. This process could have been easily implemented as the optimisation of some function and there were various plausible options that we could have adopted. Once more, seeking simplicity, we chose not to introduce a new ingredient. Individual preferences were already set according to a quantitative criterion and that same criterion could be exploited to compare them. Thus, at each step, the model built the shortcut that was the most beneficial of all, shortening paths at the regional scale.

Summarising, in the first model, called the L-L (local-local) model, node-settlements pursued their local interests relying, for their decision making, on local information. At each step, a node was extracted at random and a new link was built, connecting it to the closest one among the nodes not already connected to it. The second model, which we named the G-L (global-local) model, shared with the L-L model the fact that node-settlements pursued their local interests, but they did so basing their preferences on global (system-scale) topological and geographical information. At each step, a node was extracted at random and, among all the possible links connecting it to any other node, the one that minimised the ratio of its length to the length of the already existing shortest path will be established. Both the L-L and the G-L models are not deterministic and each run produces, in principle, a different network. In the third and last baseline model, the nodes had global information as in the G-L model, but pursued a regional scale benefit, mediating between their local preferences. At each step, the algorithm built the link associated with the (globally) minimal value of the ratio of the geodesic distance between two disconnected nodes to the length of the already existing shortest path joining them. This model is deterministic and will always generate the same network for a given set of input parameters. We named it the equitable efficiency (EE) model because of the effect of the algorithm on the global efficiency of the networks that it generates.

Besides the three baseline models, we devised a fourth one by introducing a simple modification to the EE model, thus including a version of "preferential attachment" (model EE-pa) that, in this case, was integrated in the framework of a deterministic algorithm. Without entering into technical details, the main idea was that, while in the original model all the settlements were on the same ground and the links to be built were selected among the individual preferences according to an objective and fair criterion, in the modified version the preference of nodes with more and larger links were entitled to a higher priority level. In this way, nodes with greater strength (total length of its adjacent links) tended to gather even more.

To complete the definition of the models, there was one more rule that needed to be set. It was necessary to establish a stopping condition for the creation of new links. Since the aim was to compare the networks generated by the models with the empirical ones, we considered that it was appropriate to equate their total link length. The algorithms take as input the positions of the settlements and build links between them until the total length of the connections that have been established is equal to that of all the connections in the corresponding empirical network (for an exhaustive discussion of the motivations and implications of this choice, check the previous publication by the authors, Prignano et al. 2019).

Discussion and results

Assessment of the network models
To assess whether any of the proposed generative mechanisms was likely to have shaped southern Etruria and Latium vetus TTIs, we compared model generated networks with their empirical counterparts, for each age and region. We performed such a comparison considering the network metrics that we proposed for the characterisation of terrestrial

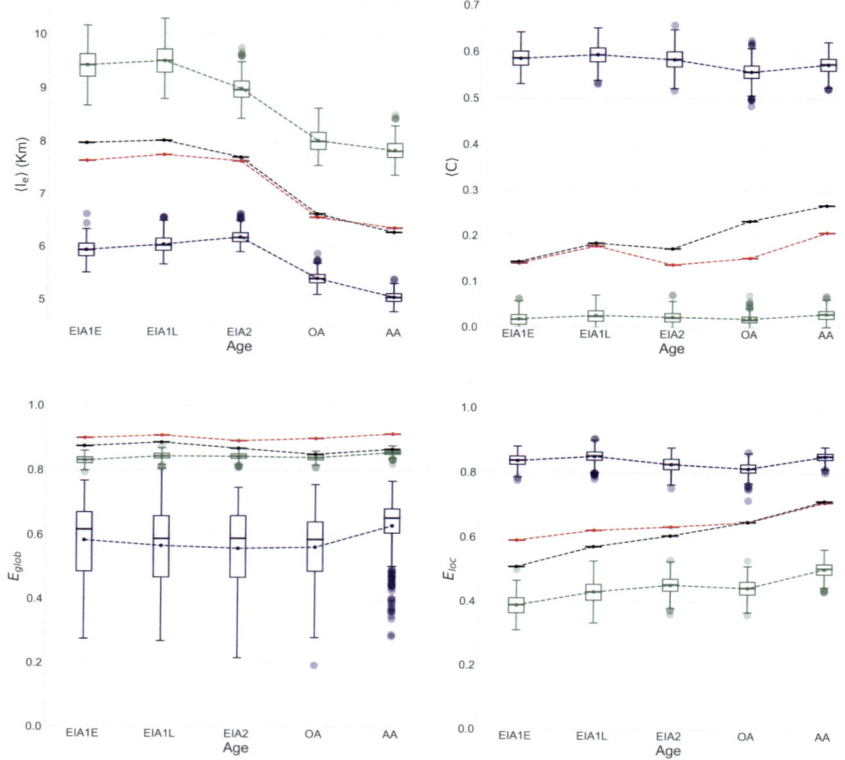

Figure 3: Etruria: comparison of the results of the calculation of characterizing measures for the empirical network and those produced by the models (black = empirical network, blue = model L-L, green = model G-L; red = model EE).

route networks. Here, we summarise the most relevant results, while a technical discussion of quantitative aspects can be found in Prignano et al. (2019) and Fulminante et al. (2017) for southern Etruria and Latium vetus, respectively.

Concerning southern Etruria, the first two models captured some of the characteristics of the empirical networks but missed some others. Specifically, the L-L model overestimated the clustering coefficient and the local efficiency and underestimated the average edge length and the global efficiency. On the other hand, the G-L model underestimated the clustering coefficient and overestimated the average edge length but is an almost perfect match for the global efficiency. On the contrary, the EE model reproduced with good accuracy all the relevant features of the empirical networks for all periods considered, with the only exception of a non-negligible difference in the clustering coefficient for the last three periods (Figure 3).

Differently from Etruria, in Latium vetus each model reproduced some of the trends of the figures of the empirical networks but always missed some others (Figure 4). In particular, the L-L model did not reproduce any of the trends of the empirical network (except for the global efficiency in two particular periods, namely EIA2 and OA). The G-L model reproduced quite well the average edge length, the local and global efficiency, but underestimated the clustering coefficient. Model EE reproduced quite well the clustering coefficient and the global efficiency (very similar to the G-L model) but underestimated the average edge length and overestimated the local efficiency. Furthermore, in the empirical networks, the heterogeneity of the node strength (measured as its standard deviation) was greater than in any model generated counterpart. Adding a tuneable preferential attachment mechanism to the EE model (model EE-pa) enabled us to generate topologies that resembled the empirical ones more accurately, although not as accurately as the EE model did in the case of Southern Etruria.

Interpreting the quantitative results

The proposed network science approach allowed us to hypothesise basic mechanisms that could have governed the decision-making process that shaped the terrestrial route network of the two regions under study.

Our conclusion is that in likelihood all the actors involved (cities and villages) were trying to build TTIs such that it was possible to reach every place from any place through a fairly short path, not permitting the existence of poorly connected areas, which could have damaged the functioning of the settlement system (in terms of commerce, communication, and defence) at the regional scale. replace with additional text:

It is interesting to note that in a least-cost path network classification proposed by Waugh (2000), this type of network, defined 'least-cost-path to the builder', is typical of agrarian societies, where arable land is precious, or scarcely populated regions, where creating routes is too expensive. This type of network contrasts the so called 'network to the user', which connects in the quickest way each possible pair of the system and is typical of hunter-gatherer societies (Fulminante 2012). Both Latium and Etruria are definitively agrarian societies growing in complexity and probably Etruria is slightly less densely populated than Latium. A third type of network, compromising between the two above, is the 'least cost triangulation network', in which the least-cost is applied only to nearest sites, implying that connections to close sites are more important than distant ones. Interestingly we applied the Delaunay model triangulation to build Latin networks in an earlier work, and they performed rather well in term of correlation between centrality indexes and centres predicted to be important by their size (Herzog 2013). A drawback of all these models is that they assume equal rank and contemporaneous sites. We will go back to these classifications in further work on least-cost paths networks.

However, it is important here to note that while in southern Etruria, optimizing the communication in the region, seemed to be the only preoccupation of all the cities and villages, regardless their status, in Latium vetus those who had been initially favoured by their location, appeared to exploit such condition pursuing local ambitions for an even better connectivity. Nonetheless, this distinguishing element did not disrupt excessively the balance at the regional scale. Latium vetus still had a very efficient terrestrial transportation infrastructure, despite that few sites were characterised by a greater number of connections.

Latin settlements could probably afford building more heterogeneous (less equitable) TTIs thanks to the relatively large total link length of their network, which allowed them to limit the damage of a non-optimal geographical distribution of paths. It is indeed worth noticing that, even though the total link length is generally larger in Southern Etruria than Latium vetus, if properly compared – taking into account the number of nodes and their average distance (Morer et al. 2020, table 1) – the latter turns out to be considerably better connected. Consequently, implementing a rich-get-richer mechanism would have been critical for the Etruscan. We cannot say whether the equitable nature of the interactions between Etruscan

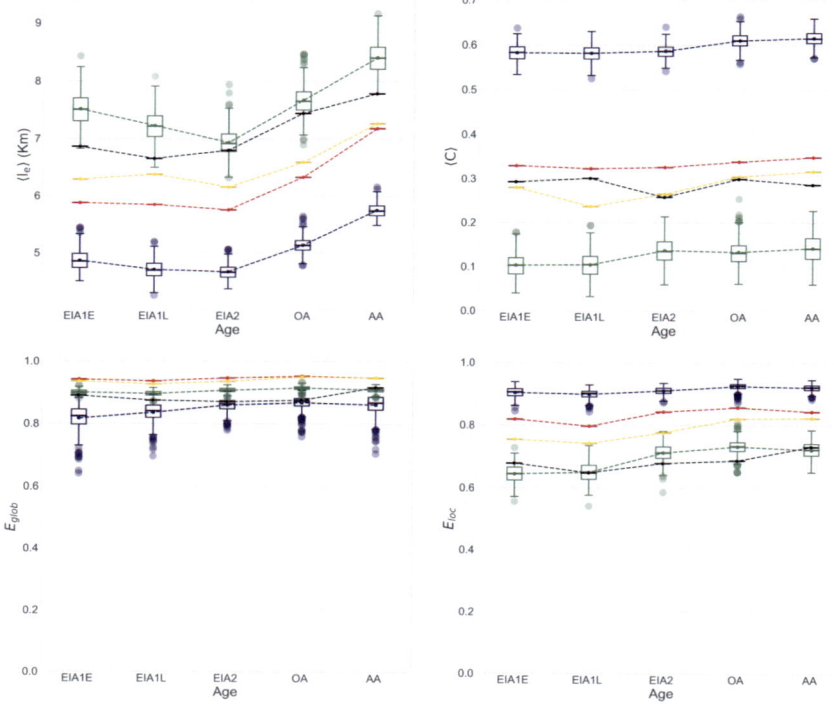

Figure 4: Latium vetus: comparison of the results of the calculation of characterising measures for the empirical network and those produced by the models
(black = empirical network, blue = model L-L, green = model G-L; red = model EE; yellow = model EE-pa).

cities made their resources scarcer (both in terms of settlement density and roads) or instead it was the other way around, uncovering this kind of causal relations is beyond the scope of our methodology. Nonetheless, our results suggest that a compact and highly connected region as Latium vetus could sustain unbalanced powers, while for Southern Etruria -a bigger and less densely populated region- power balance looked almost as the only option.

On closer inspection, we found hints that the introduction of preferential attachment as a refinement mechanism to the EE model could explain the emergence of Rome as a prominent site (see Figure 5). According to the EE-pa model, some sites, favoured by a convenient geographical position (in relation to the rest of the sites), were able (and willing) to leverage this initial advantage to increase their influence and gather even more power.

In the case of Rome, which had the greatest node strength in the empirical networks, the site happened to be also favoured by the algorithm. However, in the case of other heavily connected cities -such as Gabi- the model failed to explain their strength. At the same time, the algorithm bestowed higher strength to other sites, as for instance Satricum or the considerably less important site of Guadagnolo.[4]

---

[4] It ought to be noted here that Gabii is another primary and very important site in Latium vetus that shows clearly some specular characteristics as it will be shown in an ego-network approach that will be presented elsewhere (Fulminante et al. forthcoming); Satricum is also rather important but located in a more peripheral position; while only some sporadic Iron Age materials are known from Guadagnolo.

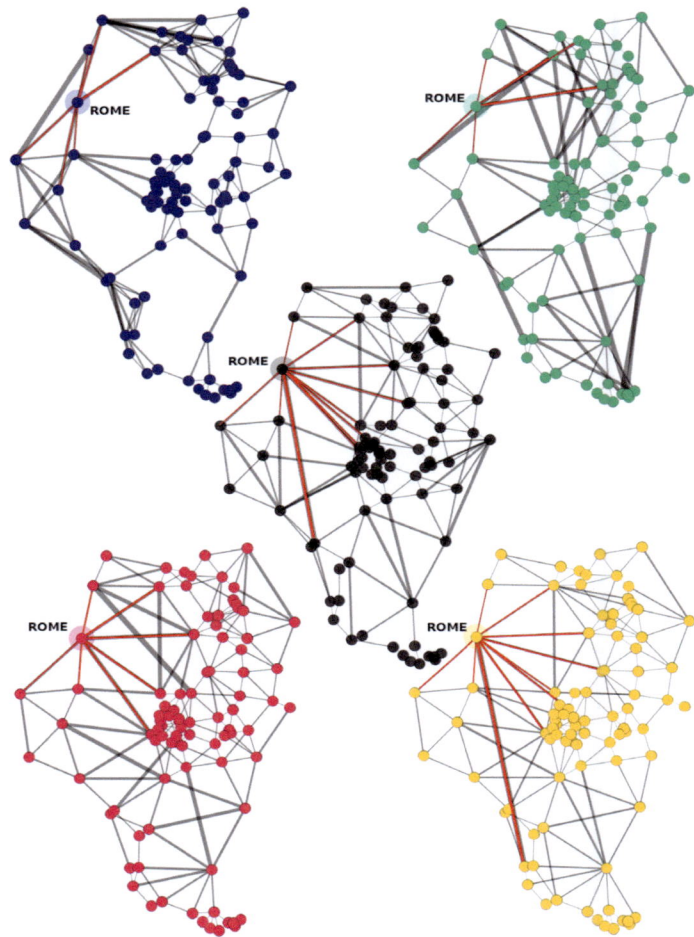

Figure 5: Latium vetus: empirical network (black) and networks produced by the models (blue = L-L, green = G-L; red = model EE; yellow = model EE-pa).

The EE-pa model reproduced a specific feature presented by Latium vetus TTI that neither the G-L model nor model EE could reproduce, that is, the existence of few sites with many distant links (Figure 5), but we did not expect it to identify who prevailed over whom or to reproduce correctly the local scale, since there were too many factors that could have determined what happened at the level of individual settlements (factors that were not included in the algorithms). Nevertheless, the apparent emergence of Rome as the most important hub of model generated networks, hints at the crucial role played by its geographical position within the system of settlements, the only attribute that the algorithm takes as an input.

The case of southern Etruria was different: there was nothing this remarkable at the local scale. Not only was the empirical node strength distribution less skewed, but the network metric itself seemed also to be almost unrelated with importance of the corresponding sites, that is, it showed lower correlation with the settlements' size (Guidi et al. forthcoming). In this case, the association between strength and power was weak, a fact that was consistent with the capacity of the EE model of reproducing the most important feature of the empirical network accurately assuming that all the nodes stood on the same ground (no preferential attachment), not considering which ones had been favoured by their position in the first steps of the algorithms. That is, possible initial advantages in terms of connectivity did not represent, in southern Etruria, a source of power imbalance and, in general, being better connected did not imply being more important.

Conclusions

In this paper we addressed the intriguing issue of the regional organisation of settlement systems through the structural analysis of their Terrestrial Transportation Infrastructures (TTI). Specifically, we proposed a methodology to contrast different hypotheses linking regional organisation of settlement systems and mechanisms shaping road network design.

To validate this novel quantitative approach, we applied it to compare two well-known neighbouring settlement systems: Southern Etruria and Latium vetus during the Iron Age. Such a comparison allowed us to highlight similarities and differences that characterise these two different complex systems, and better understand how the two systems worked. We could explore whether similarities or differences in their TTIs could reflect different socio-political systems (or, at least, different balance of power and interacting patterns within similar socio-political systems).

By means of this case study, we have shown how our proposed approach can be applied to compare different settlement systems and corroborate previously proposed hypotheses. Indeed, even though we could never be sure that we devised the best model for a given case study, it is possible to establish whether a given model works better in a certain region than in another one. Specifically, we cannot be sure that a "rich get richer" mechanism (even a weak one) did not shape Etruscan TTIs. However, we can conclude that there are higher chances that such a mechanism had an effect in shaping Latin TTIs. Generally speaking, if we have data that can be translated into networks, then generative algorithms are a good tool to understand the mechanisms that shaped those networks since they allow us to explore multiple scenarios playing the "what if?" game.

Acknowledgements

We would like to thank Helen Dawson and Francesco Iacono for inviting us to contribute to this stimulating conference and the following proceedings and Topoi for funding our participation. The research for this paper was conducted thanks to a Marie Sklodowska Curie Fellowship by Francesca Fulminante at the University of Roma Tre (Italy, Grant N 628818). The paper was developed, written and revised thanks to a fellowship at the Institute of Advanced Studies at Durham (UK, Lent Term 2017) and at the Christian-Albrechts-Universität zu Kiel (Germany, Autumn Term 2018). Discussions at those institutions respectively with Rob Witcher and Oliver Nakoinz have been most fruitful. Sergi Lozano acknowledges the financial support of Ministerio de Economia y Competitividad (MINECO) through Grant No. RYC-2012-01043. Ignacio Morer and Luce Prignano acknowledge the financial support of the European Research Council within the Advanced Grant EP-Net (340828). Every error and inaccuracy remain with the authors.

Getting around the city: A Space Syntax perspective on post-medieval Nuremberg

Donat Wehner

Human movement, street network, space syntax, regression analysis, 16th century

Movement is, without a doubt, one of the most important aspects of human activity, enabling interactions and opening up scope for agency, which in turn can be regarded as the main reasons for the persistence of cities. Cities are the biggest and most complex artefacts that humans have ever created: they consist of buildings, places, walls, canals, landmarks, neighbourhoods, and many more structural units connected by streets. In "Space Syntax Theory", material urban space is considered as a "morphological language" in which the different entities are semantically loaded elements and syntactically associated through accesses and paths. "Morphological language", therefore, can be thought of as arranged and coded space, which is understood similarly by people of similar socialisation and which has an impact on social practices and thus on human movement.[1]

Space syntax and archaeology

In archaeology and history, space syntax approaches have been primarily applied to explore the accessibility of rooms in building complexes. These include castles (Atzbach 2016; Fairclough 1992; Mathieu 1999; Meckseper 2002; Mitchell 2015), tower houses (Sherlock 2010), palaces and monumental buildings (Fisher 2014; Letesson 2014; Richardson 2003; Robb 2007) but also monasteries (Gilchrist 1994; Meckseper 2002; Thaler 2005), domestic places (Brusasco 2004; Foster 1989; Hopkins 1987; Letesson 2014; Stöger 2008, 2009), taverns (Autenrieth 2015) and even Inuit snow houses (Dawson 2000). Access analysis of building plans is connected to questions of household organisation, social

---

1   Principal exponents of space syntax theory tend to look for generalised lawful relations between physical and social space (Al-Sayed et al. 2014: 8; Hanson and Hillier 1987; Hillier and Hanson 1984: 26-27; Hillier 1996a, 1996b, 2009, 2014: 19; Franz and Wiener 2005), whereas Dafinger (2004) strengthens the idea of context- and society-sensitive dependencies, cf. also Rapoport (1982: 137).

inequality, gender roles, public and open space, liturgical actions as well as complexity, organisation and perception of space (Atzbach 2016; Autenrieth 2015; Ayán Vila et al. eds 2003; Brusasco 2004; Chatford Clark 2007; Dawson 2000; Fairclough 1992; Fisher 2014; Foster 1989; Gilchrist 1994; Hacıgüzeller and Thaler 2014; Hopkins 1987; Letesson 2014; Mathieu 1999; Meckseper 2002; Mitchell 2015; Richardson 2003; Robb 2007; Sherlock 2010; Stavroulaki and Peponis 2005; Stöger 2008, 2009; Thaler 2005). Corresponding studies of ancient cities are rather rare and concentrate on Roman and medieval times, probably because of the availability of more or less complete urban layouts. By using space syntax methods, the built environment is linked to street life, interaction and mobility and also to urban arrangements, attractiveness and developments (Craane 2013; Dhoop 2014; Kaiser 2011; Mermet and Robert 2014; Morton et al. 2012; Silvestru 2014; Stöger 2011; van Dyke 1999; van Nes 2014).

This contribution will investigate how the street network and pedestrian flows in 16th century Nuremberg were entangled[2] and what principles were followed in the patterns of human movement. In doing so, geographical space in the form of urban layouts and social space as the distribution of human encounters are bridged by space syntax theory and network analytical methods. Movement is not so much considered as a rational decision of individuals but rather under the aspect of practices in terms of social reproduction embodied in the spatial configuration of the physical environment.[3] This also means that the intensity of pedestrian flows in one space is always based on arrangements and complexities of the space in relation to other spaces or, as the American urban planner Kevin Andrew Lynch (1960: 1) stated: "Nothing is experienced by itself, but always in relation to its surroundings, the sequences of events leading up to it, the memory of past experiences".

Despite all the different approaches in archaeological and historical contributions to space syntax, they share fundamental models for movement based on the theoretical assumption that the built environment has an active role in human behaviour. Thus, on the one hand, they emphasise space as a living dimension and, on the other hand, they follow generalised ideal conceptions of human routines. The latter led to the criticism of the space syntax concept as ahistorical and spatially deterministic (Gilchrist 1994).[4] This cannot be totally dismissed. Therefore, some possibilities for better use shall be discussed. As in usual space syntax approaches, the method should be considered at first as an analytical and heuristic tool to gain new perspectives on the relation of human movement and physical space. However, the theoretical considerations on creating ideal models must not be deduced from timeless laws, but developed as social practices in their historical contexts. In addition, the ideal models should be tested against real models based on empirical data. Those correlating the closest with the empirical data should have the highest plausibility to explain patterns of human movement.

---

2   Recent empirical studies of present-day cities refer especially to a strong, often underestimated dependency of urban movement on the street network order and on the position of a street within a city (cf. Penn et al. 1998).
3   For different concepts of social practice, cf. Hillebrandt (2014) and Reckwitz (2016).
4   Further problems with space syntax applications in archaeology, such as incomplete data or the reduction of space syntax to a methodological instrument without considering theoretical aspects, are discussed by Thaler (2005: 324-326).

Space Syntax: Nuremberg as a case study

In the 16th century, Nuremberg was a prosperous city with an international sphere of action. The place functioned as a central hub in the European communication and exchange network. This is demonstrated by a map of the cartographer Erhard Etzlaub entitled "Das sein dy lantstrassen durch das Romisch reych; von einem Kunigreich zw dem andern dy an Tewtsche Land stossen von meilen zu meilen mit puncten verzeichnet wurde Getruckt von Georg glogkendon zw Nurnbergk 1501" (Etzlaub 1990), which shows

Nuremberg as a major gateway in a supra-regional road system. In addition, historical sources and numerous products from Nuremberg found in excavations in nearly all regions of the then-known world support long-distance contacts (Cassitti 2016). Furthermore, the city was one of the largest in Central Europe, with approximately 40,000 inhabitants (de Vries 1984).

The layout of Nuremberg shows two extensive areas on both sides of the Pegnitz River. Both halves seem to stand for themselves, but they are surrounded by a single complex fortification. The northern part is shaped by the castle and Saint Sebaldus Church, the southern part by Saint Lawrence Church. The arterial streets extending from the main gates are focused in this direction. The widely visible monumental buildings appear at the same time as landmarks in the city layout.

The function and appearance of the city in the 16th century suggest that accessibility of central nodes as well as effective transit traffic may have played an important role. Both hypotheses will be tested by transferring them into models.

Figure 1: Ground plan of Nuremberg, Pfinzing-Atlas 1588-1598 (from Pfinzing 1588).

The applied space syntax method is based on a radical reduction of the city. The basis is page 8 from the so-called Pfinzing-Atlas showing the layout of Nuremberg (Figure 1). It was mapped by Nuremberg's cartographer Paul Pfinzing, the Elder, who reverted to the oldest city layout design from 1555 - the so-called Nöttelein map - which itself is based on a wooden model from around 1540. In contrast to his precursors, Pfinzing arranged the city layout by using various colours marking quarters, dividing different areas or highlighting single buildings. In doing so, he transfers - just like in space syntax theory - the complex structure of the urban space into a kind of simplified language, enabling the viewer to capture the structure and setting of Nuremberg. In addition, readability was increased by adding labels for streets, places and public buildings (cf. Schiermeier 2006: 66-69; 78-79).

This again helps us in georeferencing the city layout. By using the first scaled cadastral map of Nuremberg published in 1811 (Schiermeier 2006: 114), housing blocks and public space can be localised and rectified to obtain an image that reflects the street network of 16th-century Nuremberg as accurately as possible (Figure 2). In the next step, the urban street network is transferred into an axial map (Figure 3).[5]

Movement possibilities are represented, on the one hand, by vectors running around barriers, such as housing blocks or separate buildings, and, on the other hand, by connecting the public space as a whole.[6] This way, the complex structure of the city is presented as a compilation of linear connections allowing a precise description of urban space: the axial map can be depicted as a kind of a structural urban fingerprint. Since it is based on algorithms following fixed rules, this approach guarantees the traceability of the model by other scientists as well as its structural comparability and contrast with complex networks of other cities' public space, as long as the same algorithms are used.[7]

Understanding the lines as nodes and their crossings as edges in a network, ratios of the potentials of human movement and social interaction can be identified and visualised. They are derived by connection patterns of streets and places.

A space syntax measure, referring to the accessibility of urban space, is provided by an integration equation, which in network analytical terms is denoted as "closeness" (Figure 4).

It is a centrality measure, mathematically described as the sum of the length of the shortest paths between one node and all other nodes in the network.

$$Integration(i) = \frac{N}{\sum_y d(y,i)},$$

where N represents the total number of nodes in the network and $d(y,i)$ the distances between the nodes y and i.

A node - in our case a line representing public space like a street or place - is more central the closer it is to all the others in the network. The higher the integration of a

---

[5] All computations have been performed with the spatial network analysis software depthmap and the geographic information system QGIS 2.14.

[6] For further backgrounds see Hillier and Hanson (1984); Hillier (2014); Turner et al. (2001), for the algorithm used and nuances of the definition see Turner et al. (2005) and for some unsolved problems see Ratti (2004).

[7] This kind of formalisation and topological display of cities has often led to the accusation that it does not meet the complexity of urbanism (cf. Netto 2016; Soja 2001). This is true for the richness of beliefs, ideas and values, but to capture patterns of complexity, focusing on quantity could be extremely useful.

Figure 2: Georeferenced and rectified public space of 16th-century Nuremberg (credit: Donat Wehner).

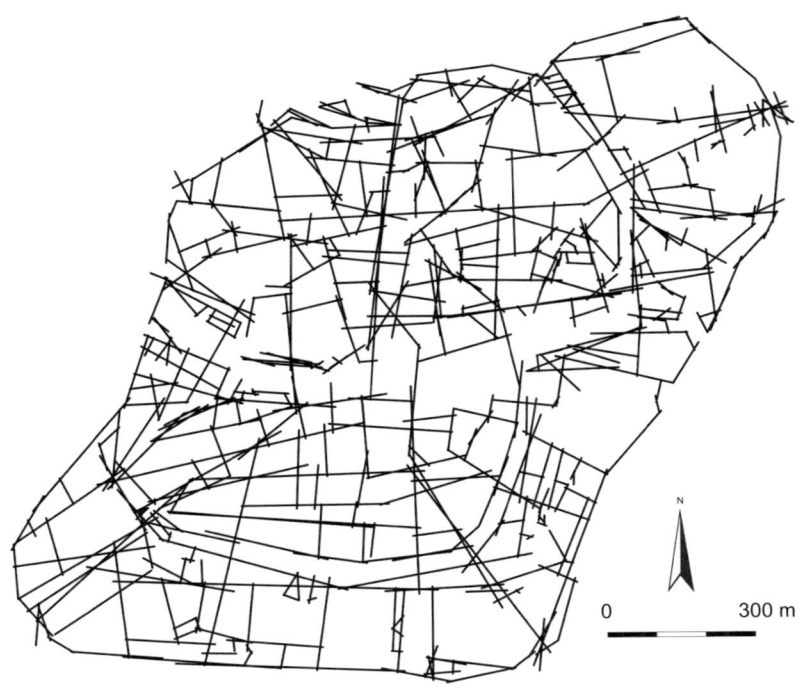

Figure 3: Axial map of Nuremberg's public space in the 16th century (credit: Donat Wehner).

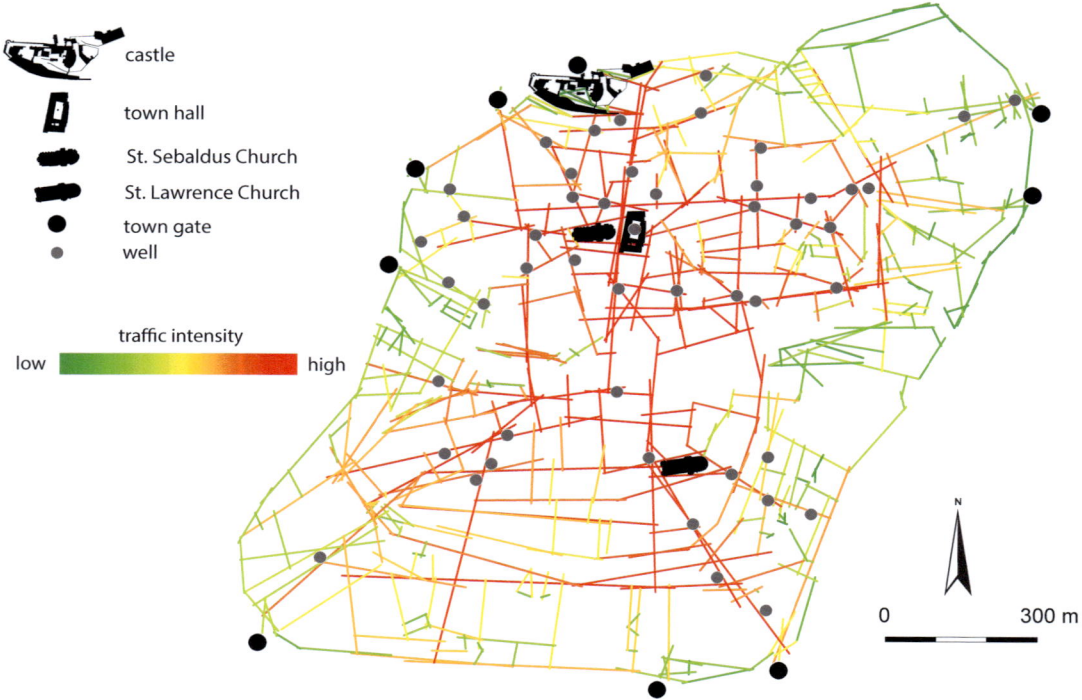

Figure 4: Ideal spatial layout accessibility model => integration (credit: Donat Wehner).

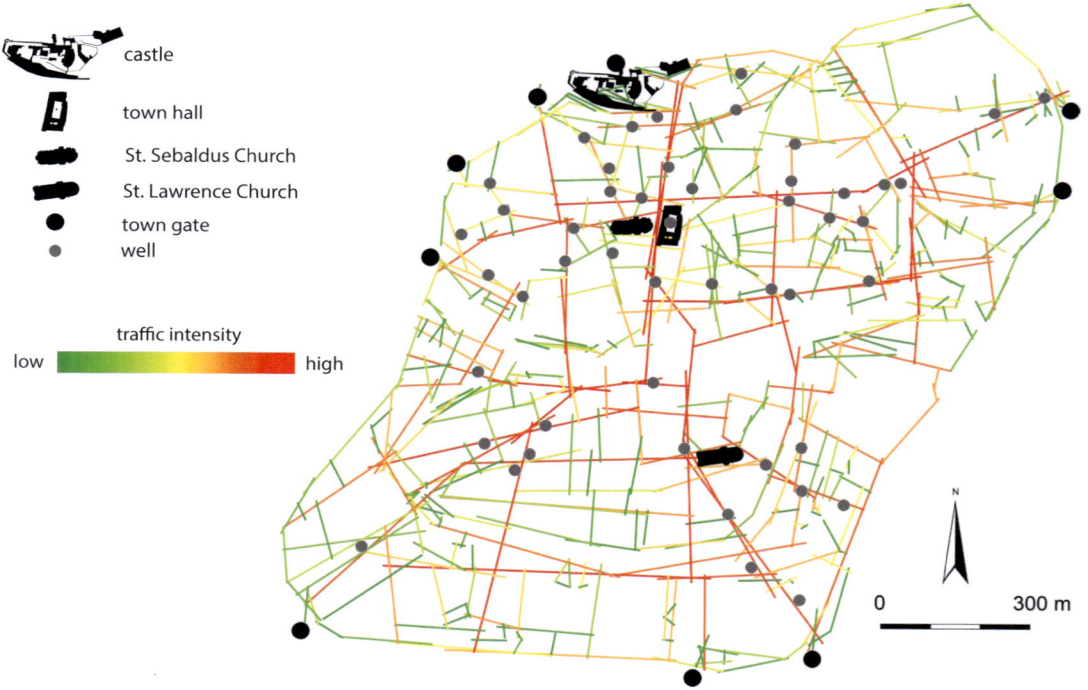

Figure 5: Ideal spatial layout accessibility model => choice (credit: Donat Wehner).

node, the easier is the access to other nodes. Through nodes with high integration, things and information can be distributed and received swiftly (Nakoinz 2013d: 107; Trappmann et al. 2011: 48). If the principle of accessibility was crucial for human movement patterns in 16th-century Nuremberg, there was probably a considerable amount of traffic especially in the city centre and near the castle.

The connection of urban places in respect of the transit traffic is best identified by a space syntax measure called "choice", which equals "betweenness" in network analytical terminology (Figure 5). Choice is described as the number of shortest paths crossing a node i divided by the number of all shortest paths between all node pairs in the network.

$$Choice(i) = \frac{N_{shortest\ paths\ through\ i}}{N_{all\ shortest\ paths}}$$

Nodes with a high choice value connect subgroups of node pairs in a network. The choice measure is especially feasible for street networks regarding the transport system because it is in principle based on reaching nodes as fast or as energy-efficiently as possible (Barthélemy 2011: 8-9; Nakoinz 2013d: 107-108). The ideal model of spatial layout accessibility regarding the aspect of choice shows several axes for 16th century Nuremberg with high traffic running west-east and south-north.

Whether the movement principles of integration and choice really played a role cannot be judged by the ideal models alone. Because an empirical counting of pedestrians is not possible for Early Modern Nuremberg, a step depth model shall be implemented in which the

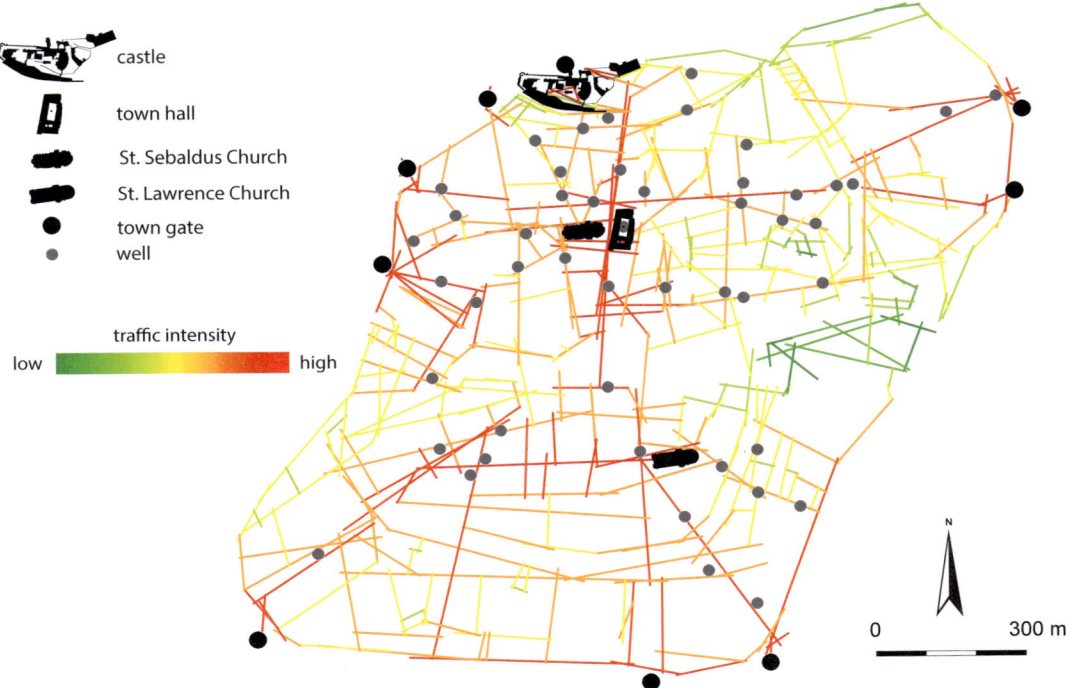

Figure 6: Real spatial layout accessibility model => step depth (credit: Donat Wehner).

accessibility of known major interaction hubs, such as Saint Sebaldus Church, the town hall, the central market, the castle, Saint Lawrence Church and the town gates, are captured.

Ideal versus real models

The degree of accessibility of one network segment towards a destination is measured by the number of network segments that must be crossed. In contrast to theoretical ideal models, this model is called a "real" spatial layout model. A refinement could be reached by considering physical efforts to overcome distances, background noises or fields of vision and smells (for modelling bodily experiences see the contributions in White and Surface-Evans (2012), and for computing soundscapes see Luick (2016) or Schwesinger (2017)). Moreover, an extension into 3D space might contribute to an improvement of such models.[8] These components are not considered here in order not to overcomplicate the procedure and its comprehensibility.

A comparison with the black coloured public space of Nuremberg shows that the pedestrian flow is estimated as very high especially in areas where the streets are very broad (Figure 7). This can be seen as another argument for the correctness of the model.

Now the comparison of the ideal models with the real model is of interest. As an additional cross-reference, wells have been mapped besides the central interaction hubs such as churches, the castle and gates (Figure 4-6). They may as well be seen as a proxy for high traffic volumes because their position must have been accessible to many people. In addition, many wells were highly decorated, and thus deliberately placed on highly frequented streets and places, so as to be noticed by as many people as possible. Belonging to the best-known wells, the "Beautiful fountain" at the edge of the central market is one of the main attractions of the city even today although its form has changed (Zintl 1993).

Comparing the distribution of wells with the ideal models, the integration model seems to show insufficient traffic in the areas near the western, southern and eastern city walls and excessive traffic in the city centre (Figure 4). The choice model also reflects insufficient density in the centre of the city (Figure 5). The real step depth model fits the distributions of the wells best, as was expected (Figure 6). Should both ideal models be rejected and declared useless to explain human movement in 16th-century Nuremberg? Taking every model individually, the answer must be yes. Nonetheless, it should not be assumed that only the accessibility factor of the integration model or the traversability factor dealt with in the choice model were crucial for movement patterns in 16th-century Nuremberg. In fact, both factors might have played a role (Figure 8).

This can be confirmed by combining both ideal models. This comes a lot closer to the real traffic model than each ideal model on its own. Similar to the real model (Figure 6), the ideal overall model shows a high traffic potential for streets running towards gates. Furthermore, the area around the axe between the castle, Saint Sebaldus church, the town hall, the central market and Saint Lawrence Church is attractive for pedestrian and vehicle movement just as in the real model.

---

8   Taking into account the ground plan alone has been often criticised, for example, by Hohmann-Vogrin (2005: 287) or Ratti (2004). Initial efforts to combine space syntax concepts with 3D space are made by Paliou (2014), Papadopoulos and Earl (2014), and Schroder et al. (2007).

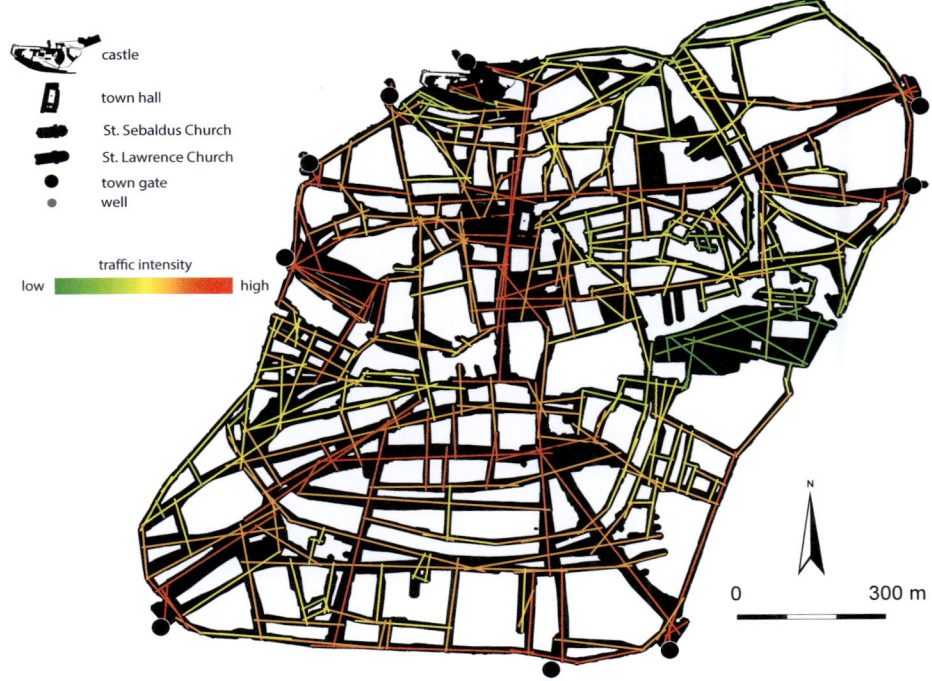

Figure 7: Comparison of the step depth model with the street width (credit: Donat Wehner).

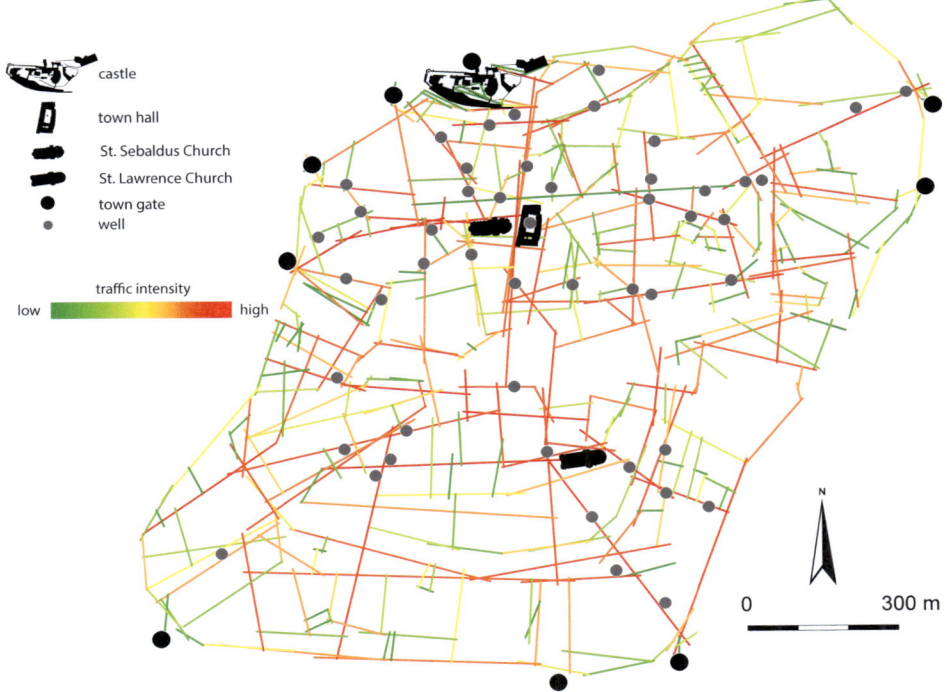

Figure 8: Combining the ideal models => integration*choice (credit: Donat Wehner).

In conclusion, testing the ideal model against the real one leads to the assumption that both accessibility and traversability factors of the choice model co-determined the movement patterns in 16th-century Nuremberg.

The integration model supports the idea that the configurations of the street network directed the traffic especially towards the representative buildings and the central market (Figure 4). The castle, the town hall, the market and the big churches were situated in such a way that they could be reached from all different places in the city. The latter stood right in the centre of movement flows, while the castle seems to have drawn movement towards itself but was not directly affected by it.

Regarding the choice model, it is striking that it shows intensive traffic for arterial streets (Figure 5). Nuremberg's street network seems to be built in a way that guides human movement towards the gates, channelling traffic in and out of the city and seldom towards impassable parts of the city walls. This confirms the hypothesis of the choice model that an effective traversing of Nuremberg was important for movement in the city. Thus, urban performance correlates well with Nuremberg's role as a long distance trading place reflected by a global networking pattern in the local street network.

In order to refine this, it should be added that of course not every pattern of human movement can be derived from the configuration of the street network. To indicate this,

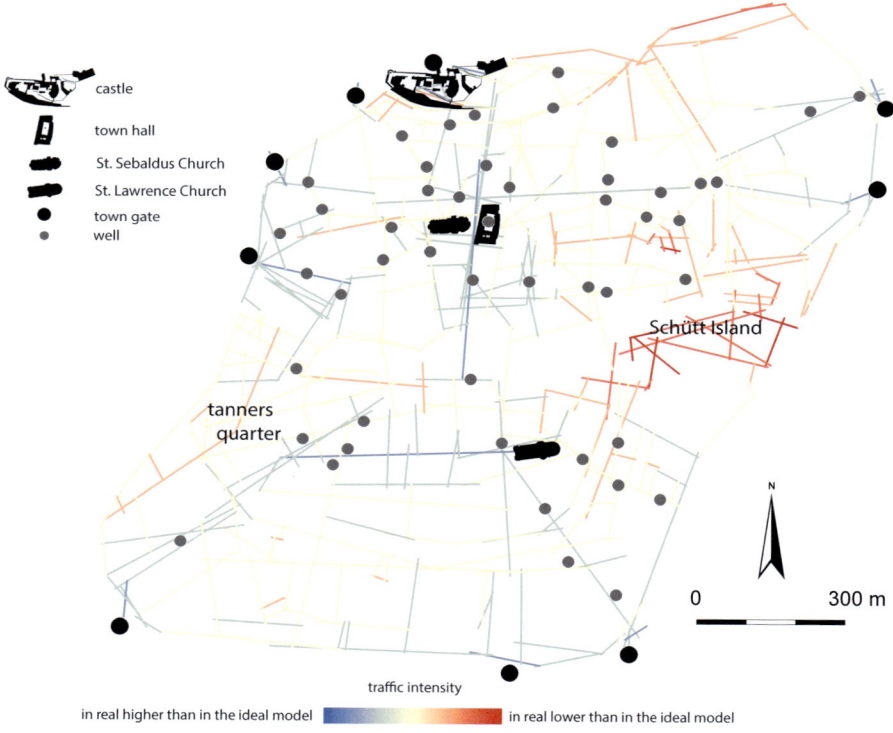

Figure 9: With regression analysis, the correlations and discrepancies of the ideal choice*integration model (dependent variable) and the real step depth model (independent variable) can be visualized (credit: Donat Wehner).

a regression analysis is used to estimate and visualise relations between the combined ideal choice-integration model and the real step depth model (Figure 9).

The result shows that the ideal model based on the street system configuration predicts partly too little and partly too much traffic. In the areas in which the traffic seems to be more intensive in the real model, the difference is less intense and therefore less problematic. Conversely, there are public spaces that are highly overrated by the ideal model. This concerns the sparsely populated "Schütt Island", which was used as a waste disposal site, and the archaeologically investigated tanner's quarters (Lorenz 2010). Regarding these activities, both areas seem unattractive to human movement. This supports the view that land use patterns are an additional important influencing factor for the intensity of pedestrian flows and social interaction.

Urban spatial networks and human movement behaviour in urban spaces: Conclusion

In conclusion, it can be noted that the spatial street network order complemented by other facilities can be proved as a coded arrangement reproducing rules and norms of human movement in the city. Based on theoretical approaches for 16th-century Nuremberg, it is assumed that movement followed the principles of effective transit and destination traffic. The hypothesis was transferred into computer-based models and tested. In general, it could be verified. But some areas, such as the tanner's quarters or "Schütt Island", do not fit into the ideal movement pattern by the premises of effective transit and destination traffic. For the future, it would be useful to expand these models by multimodal approaches to test a variety of assumptions on movement patterns in a city.[9] Moreover, individual based models, which simulate the localities visited by individuals or the time different people spent at and between the localities, would be also of interest (cf. Perkins et al. 2014). Furthermore, it is advisable to include other urban performance parameters in addition to the street grid while modelling urban movement, such as land use, the height of buildings, building materials, entrance types or façade designs, etc.

Let us have a final look at the map of Nuremberg, which stood at the beginning of the analysis (Figure 1). In light of the map, the question must be posed if a space syntax perspective was even needed for the conclusion that transit and destination traffic played an important role in 16th-century Nuremberg. This is probably not strictly necessary given the fact that - for this period - comparable, generalised suggestions on the city as a traffic-space already exist (Kaufhold 2001: 31-34). Nevertheless, space syntax turns out to be a useful approach in a number of ways. For one, it seeks to understand the embodiment of practices in the material world by emphasising social reproduction through a network perspective of social processes and spatial arrangements. The close intertwining of relational space, materiality and daily life has become only recently a central issue of humanities and social sciences traded under the names of "spatial" and "material turn"

---

9   Suggestions can be found, for example, in Jiang (2009). Although not from the field of archaeology or history, the monograph of the physicists Philippe Blanchard and Dimitri Volchenkov from Bielefeld with the title "Mathematical Analysis of Urban Spatial Networks" is remarkably useful. In contrast to the archaeological and historical contributions using very limited techniques, they present a broad variety of formal methods from graph theory, probability theory and statistical physics to analyse networks of urban space (Blanchard and Volchenkov 2009; see also Volchenkov and Blanchard (2008). For further modelling approaches of urban infrastructure networks see also Barthélemy and Louf (2017) and Batty (2013).

(*e.g.* Döring and Thielmann 2009; Latour 2007; Löw 2015; Stockhammer and Hahn 2015). However, reflections and investigations on how spatiality and materiality are related to social phenomena are still rare. On this matter, space syntax with its pragmatic and empiric focus can provide a decisive impulse. In concrete terms, it can be used as a theoretical and application-oriented method to explore urban movement as an essentially social practice, enabling a more precise description of complex urban entanglements as an action context than would be possible by just looking at the city layout. Transferring configurations of street networks as an expression of movement patterns into ratios increases the comprehensibility and simplifies comparability to other urban movement patterns. Consider, for instance, how a corresponding analysis of several other cities of the 16th century, taking into account temporal dynamics, could provide solutions for the controversial issue of the dimensions of inner-city structural rearrangements in Central Europe, caused by radically changing long-distance trading networks due to the discovery of the so-called New World at the beginning of Early Modern times.

Memory as a network of affects

Bridging the humanities and social sciences to understand the social spaces of storytelling

Sarah De Nardi

Place, identity, traumascapes, heritage values, historic landscapes

Introduction

This chapter explores how various human and non-human agencies shape the ways in which three different social and cultural groups construct, 'feel', remember and relate to recent histories and remote pasts interconnectedly. Interconnectedness, in this sense, is a relationship of reciprocal growth and influence in which multiple agents (human and non-human) feed on each other and draw upon each other's affordances to function as a system. Community is such an example. I especially draw on Pauketat's idea that communities should be framed as a "quality of places, experiences, practices and even human bodies" (2008: 249) – a holistic and multi-agency entity. The book's broad themes of socialisation of space and 'relatedness' come into their own in my approach to these linked-up workings through the lens of more-than-representational frames – affect, memory and the imagination. These are networks of affects and memory that are profoundly socially-embedded and shifting in the social and political consciousness of groups as much as they are intensely felt emotionally and through the body. They are also closely linked to temporality and place, two intrinsic factors shaping affects, memories, and the imaginaries of individuals and communities.

I present in turn three accounts of how communities shape heritage as a coalescing process of reciprocal growth and understanding. I turn to Italy, northern England and the Northwestern frontier of Pakistan. By thinking of place and identity as networked affects, we may glean a deeper understanding of how place feels and how these communities and social-cultural groups interpret and feel about their surroundings. We could apply our analytical lens on storytelling – the construction and enactment of dynamic narratives and representations of the past into the present – and on memory – the more-than-representational channel for facts, imaginings and interpretations of the past in the present.

If we understand a social network as a structure made up of individuals (or organisations) called "nodes", then these nodes are connected by one or more specific types of interdependence, such as friendship, kinship, common interest, financial exchange, like and dislike, sexual relationships, or relationships of belief, knowledge or prestige (Sparrowe et al. 2001; Geys and Murdoch 2010). This kind of multifaceted relationship does not stop at human beings of flesh and blood: the dead, and legendary figures, lay urgent claim to a presence in significant and meaningful networks of relationships tethered to spaces and places – one of the key concerns of the present book.

We know that there can be many kinds of ties (or links, or connections) between nodes, ties which are often unpredictable and undetectable through canonical analyses of space and/or socialisation. Moreover, research emerging in several academic fields has shown that social networks operate on many levels, from the familial up to the national and global level (*e.g.* Girman and Newman 2002; McPherson et al. 2001). What interests me the most about social network theory is both its randomness and its focus on agency. As someone without a background in social network scholarship, I am drawn to the idea that a network plays a critical role not only in what social and topographical patterns emerge and develop, but also how (and what) 'problems' come into being. This seems to me a novel way of exploring old problems to do with social competition and political feuding – something which occupies a large part of my research and thinking. I am convinced by data showing that networks also determine the way problems are solved, and the degree to which 'nodes' succeed in achieving their goals in the midst of multiple 'unfoldings' (Diani and McAdam 2003). A network can also be used to measure social capital – the value that an individual gets from the social network, and their legacy – how they are remembered. Memory theorists (e.g. Halbwachs 1992) consider memories as the embodied accomplishments of agents in a complex world – in a complex network of overlapping and divergent knowledge and imaginations, I would add. From shared memory, "we pass by degrees to collective memory and in commemorations linked to places consecrated by tradition. It is the occurrence of such experiences that first introduced the notion of sites of memory, prior to the expressions […] that have subsequently become attached to this expression" (Ricoeur 1981: 149).

Storytelling

Post-modern narratives and the writing of histories as opposed to an authoritative 'History' resonate with contemporary preoccupations about multivocality and identity across the Historical and social sciences, from Dominick LaCapra (2001) to Michel de Certeau (1984) just to cite a couple. A heightened reflexivity on the practice of historiography foregrounds the present-ness of those past events (and their affect/effect on potential futures): open-ended, intermingled and creating dizziness rather than closure. This powerful mechanism of 'opening' up historical narratives is effected through a focus on storytelling. Storytelling is a way into affectual, interpersonal and tangible or intangible networks; telling a story is a sharing and a making, a mode of exploration of memory and senses of place and of the past across cultural domains. The act of storytelling as a cultural performance can be understood in terms which Alessandro Portelli aptly sums up as "history, myth, ritual and symbol" (2003: 38).

Past happenings and their meanings are discursively produced, transmitted and mediated. It may be important to note the potent interconnected linkages between past and present, between long-ago materialities and imagined futures, which in themselves form networks transcending time and materiality. A recollection of the past, a frayed old memento, or a particularly heartfelt story, can feel more present and powerful than a contemporary artefact. For Waterton and Watson, "human connections to the past are [...] tangible, and have a materiality upon which they depend that makes them objects of heritage" (2010: 2). Heritage – in the way I use it in this paper – is something that people 'feel' and 'do' as part of their everyday lives, partaking in the emotional network of materiality and stewardship. In the sections that follow I explore the hybrid and many-sided nature of affectual networks of memory and sense of place through the lens of storytelling.

Multivocality in war and post-conflict narratives is crucial to their development, social spread and understanding. Over the years, my oral history work with communities in Italy who experienced or remember the Second World War and the armed resistance struggle of 1943-1945 has produced stories mediated not only by the body, but also by the cultural-emotional networks in which they are produced, enacted, shared. Stories, which may be framed as embodied and socialised performances of an individual's or community's shared memory, co-produce knowledge and feeling - stories constitute a thing in the present, forming networks that reach out from a past to shape many possible networked 'todays' and 'tomorrows'. This proactive interpersonal process could be thought of as a form of popular knowledge as well as academic knowledge, because it defines the cultural belonging and sense of identity of the interviewee and of the community and social network to which the 'node' belongs.

Italy: The networked traumascapes of the Second World War

In my research with veterans (2009-2013), I explored their engagement with places and persons during the Resistance and occupation. I used original and secondary archival sources and oral history interviews (conducted by myself and others) to explore the ways in which identities were performed and how strongly actors were linked with certain locales by their identity, and what role they had played within a certain social and affectual network. Second World War memory in Italy is shaped and negotiated by the interactions of often incompatible and unexpected nodes, establishing and negotiating mnemonic and political ties that exceed historiographic accuracy. Divided memories of the war constitute networks of identity and political consciousness in Italy to this day (Mammone 2006) transmitted and enacted through educational storytelling in schools and media debate (newspapers, blogs). The social and cultural legacy of the Second World War is ever more prominent 70 years after the end of the conflict. It is what Waterton and Watson call a "process": a process that is "linked to memory, identity, politics, place, dissonance and performance" (2010: 4); these may be all construed as elements of a networked sense of place.

Articulated through the social, negotiated in a network of meanings, storytelling about the war affects places and their person-thing-memory entanglements in the everyday. This is a process affecting many, not just at the individual level. In northern Italy in particular, war and resistance-related storytelling is a performative act that unites members of an ingroup (the former partisans and their allies) and alienates others (those who had an allegiance to the Fascists ideals of Mussolini and his legacy). Despite these differences, and the various contexts in which they operate, storytellers act in social spheres of a certain reach: schools, the web, cultural associations. While firmly framed in present socialisations (attendance to ceremonial commemorations, blog activism, school outreach activities), both mnemonic networks still actively communicate a certain version of the past. Drawing on the work of DeLanda (2006), Anderson (2006) and Deleuze and Guattari (2004) among others, Harris asserts the utility of approaching and reframing "community" as not only "made up of humans but also of things, places, animals, plants, houses and monuments" (2014: 77). Here, I would add stories and memories to that list – the intangible elements that can make and break communities.

Although memory of the war is firstly a singular act of recollection, the proximity and communality of experience within a group (say, veteran partisans, a town, a region) make sense of individual memories and create a viable, shared experience in that "imagined community" (after Anderson 2006, in Harris 2014), leading to a mutually-agreed and respected version of the past. Stories of fratricidal violence, of ambushes, of killings, do much more than just structuring and representing content – they move, emerge, and affect us in the very act of telling. Stories may also perturb, 'other', and divide. The ethnographic encounter with war veterans and their families, as we shall see, engenders much more than data or evidence for a story already established. Fieldwork with people and their 'things' represents a "collapse of the experience/analysis divide, such that the experience of things in the field is already an encounter . . . with meanings" (Henare et al. 2007: 4).

Interpersonal perception of individuals and communities shaped the way that the war was perceived then, and how it is remembered now. Past and present political identities shape an everyday politics of social inclusion and exclusion that is relational, dependent on context and 'audience', and yet deeply interconnected (De Nardi 2016). The politics of storytelling makes up what Whittle, in the context of the European Neolithic, has called "moral communities" powered by shared values and emotions (Whittle 2003, in Harris 2014). These notions are useful to an understanding of how mnemonic social networks and their performativity are enacted in Italy. Here, in the post-war period, the emphatic insistence on the dehumanisation of the Fascists by their anti-Fascist (and largely Communist) antagonists in the war and beyond is discussed at length in Claudio Pavone's treatise *A Civil War* (1991) [2014]. The author – a former anti-Fascist partisan – deconstructs the stimuli and motives leading to the establishment and events of the armed resistance movement into three overlapping categories of patriotic war, class war and civil war. Needless to say, Pavone's book has not proved popular with fringes of the Italian Left and veteran partisan groups.

The memories of the victors, the victims and the perpetrators in the Italian civil war blend, merge, converge and sharply diverge depending on who is listening to the stories being told. Each specific audience's mood and political and ideological makeup will determine how the story is received. And often, the nature of the audience will actually shape the content of the memory being relayed, if the teller wished to avoid confrontation and contestation.

In mainstream pro-resistance narratives, the act of ideological dehumanising of the Fascists in storytelling led to their exclusion from the emotional geographies of home and homeland has served multiple purposes. In the shaping of national and regional emotional and affective networks, punishing the Fascists with a negation of their Italian identity was the climax of the post-war recriminations at the failed arrest and prosecution for war crimes of many ex-Blackshirts. In the partisans' storytelling, attempts to dehumanise the Fascists have also reached beyond the close-knit community of original rememberers. Dehumanising and negating the national pride of Fascists has protected Italians from facing a very unsavoury fact: that even the affable nature of the Catholic Italians was capable of betrayal and arbitrary violence. It seemed less daunting to construe an image of the armed resistance as purely a struggle through which Italians attempted and succeeded in ejecting the 'Other' par excellence – the Wehrmacht (not to mention the SS). It may also be argued that the memory of a war against a foreign enemy is not as traumatic as the memory of fellow villagers turning against each other. An analytics focusing on identity practices may allow us to understand wartime events and attitudes in terms of overarching local traditions and perceptions. For example, long-held grudges against Austrians and German-speakers in the greater Veneto region after the Great War (Vendramini 1984: 175) may go some way towards explaining why the populace hated the Germans even when they were still Axis allies, or why the majority of Italians mistrusted and rejected German-speaking soldiers even when they behaved fairly (Pavone 1991: 206).

Furthermore, memory takes place in a social and cultural framework negotiated and shared by a wider mnemonic community of people. The memories may indeed differ and even clash; but we are dealing with specific networked, shared, negotiated events and places and people regularly recall fondly, or fearfully, with regret, or with an endless melancholic sense of loss. The workings of partial memory and deliberate rejection or forgetting of the civil war tearing apart Italian communities belong to the realm of the more-than-representational – to a network of affects and shifting sense of place. They cannot be narrated or examined in isolation. The mutual support and encouragement of other nodes in a mnemonic community, despite the integral reluctance to absorb or even engage with the political opposition's counter-memory, create enduring affects that give a sense and a meaning to a past, to a present and ultimately, to future social networks of belonging. Whether good or bad, memory of the war serves as a badge of social bond and social visibility – enacted in the storytelling and sharing of "I was there" memories – but also as a mechanism of belonging and a measure of success or failure.

Beamish Museum: Networks of affects through time

I now turn to a different context. From the organic memory of Italian communities after the Second World War, I turn to the strategies for integrating 'staged' memories and unrehearsed memories at an open-air museum of the coal mining communities of northern England. Indeed, the poetics of heritage co-production behaves like a network bringing together and bridging nodes such as heritage publics, practitioners and heritage objects. This poetics occurs not only through direct memory, or eyewitness accounts (like in Italy) but also through materiality and the imagination. Co-production of heritage values relies on sensory clues exceeding the representational. Here, I examine the role of autobiographies and the senses in the social and spatial experience at Beamish open air museum in County Durham, in the Northeast of England (Figure 1). By reflecting on data from oral history focus groups and collaborative mapping, I identify some of the social network formations and interactions with object replicas or building reconstructions occurring in this living-history museum. In understanding Beamish Museum, we may take as a starting point Ricoeur›s notion of our ability to "reach out" to others via stories using "imagination and sympathy", powerful emotional events dictating our experience in every aspect of everyday lives – especially socialisation.

Figure 1: Beamish Museum street scene (credit: wikicommons).

"Museum objects [...] are perceived by both museum workers and users to represent something from the past; they are perceived as representations of some activity, person, or event. As documents then, museum objects are involved in *communication*." (Wood and Latham 2009: 4, my emphasis).

The Northeast of England is a deindustrialised region characterised by a keen sense of what it *used* to be, not what it is. The decline of the coal mining industry, in successive bouts of mine closures across Tyneside and County Durham, is still perceived today as the neglect of the Government in looking after the local communities' livelihood. In 1973, in the midst of the waning coalmines, a blueprint for an outdoor museum in County Durham was conceived. The museum was born around a temporal node: the year 1913. The idea was to work around the last two generations of local memory.

Affective and sensorially-informed ways of knowing, learning and socialising *in place* take centre stage at the museum, above and beyond the case for or against its authenticity and educational mileage. The Museum's popularity among the residents of the North-east (and beyond) is sensational. This process could correspond to what Andrea Witcomb (2003) calls the 'irrational power of museums'. We might conceive of such irrational power as a channelling and manifestation of powerful networks of affect circulating throughout Beamish: through the costumed reenactors, visitors, the mundane and humble everyday objects exhibited in the museum grounds and the recreated, staged and reconstructed buildings and structures that form its architectural and environmental milieu.

If the visitors' attunement to the *familiarity* of the vernacular engenders interconnected and interpersonal affects, then Beamish Museum enables rich, physical and emotional attunements for many visitors – a "moral community" of sorts among locals and visitors. Linkages with other times and other lives are encouraged and stimulated by the immersive setting through the senses (see also Classen and Howes 2006). An affective connection, an intangible yet moving tethering to networks of nostalgia and longing, is accomplished through comparison and recognition, involving objects both present in the exhibition and others remembered and imagined by visitors. Authenticity, Ouzman suggests, is directional. "Some people are more concerned with the object as material manifestation while others are more interested in the knowledge and emotions tethered to objects" (2006: 274).

For instance, I was interested in whose knowledge was tied to the post-war prefabricated Airey Houses, the Grand Electric cinema, the Middlesbrough hairdressers' parlour, and Esther G.'s Sunderland semi-detached council house due a new lease of life through Remaking Beamish. As 'objects', the reassuring and often mundane look of the buildings and objects therein may seem inconspicuous to those who visit the forthcoming 1950s Town. Apart from perhaps the Grand Electric Cinema's promise of retro cinematic fun, the town's familiarity might not seem 'interesting' enough to get excited about. We might then ask what the audiences will make of it – its mundane and rather unglamorous materiality in the museum setting. And yet, the mesh of familiar scenes, the emotions and responses the various settings will evoke in visitors, will draw people in its make-believe world. A past suspended in the present, the stage Northeast 1950s may well lure visitors to its network of imaginaries and emotions, through familiarity. Familiarity may act as a shared emotional genealogy of its material culture, storytelling and autobiographical reflection. Each reconstructed brick is a link in a potent network of what makes the 1950s past *feel* relevant today through a sense of a shared past and shared values in a moral community of locals. If storytelling and stories were the imaginative and tangible ties of sense of identity and place in post-war Italy, the materiality of everyday domestic objects serves as a networked mechanism of unity and shared remembrance at museums such as the Beamish.

Objects

Objects may reveal the continuity of social and cultural identity through time. They may do so by providing foci of involvement in the present, mementoes and souvenirs of the past, and signposts to the future. That is why, on occasion, it is so very hard to let go of things, however awkward, that belonged to someone we loved and lost. There is a sense that part of the deceased owner or user still somewhat reside in the material, the shape and the smell of an object. The ineffable essence of the absent other (or non-absent past, after Domanska 2005) haunts us, making it difficult to dispose of stuff we normally would not want in our homes. For some, "every property is a *condensed story*. To describe the properties of materials is to tell the stories of what happens to them as they flow, mix and mutate" (Classen and Howes 2007: 14). And yet, stories circulate in objects, rather than preserving or containing them. They are dynamic. Any museum donation does not solely consist in the physical object itself at but is a complex whole of which the thing is just one element in "a molecule of interconnecting [equally important] pieces of information" (Parry 2007: 80).

Objects loom large on the way that we live networked *past-leaning, affected* lives. It is not difficult to speculate on their role as networks of affect in a regional society, bound up with the references to past times and with expectations of shared cultural performances in the 'heritage' arena (see also Harvey 2001). Donating personal belongings that live in a liminal state between 'cherished' and 'unwanted' to Beamish is a part of this networked love affair. From parlour to attic to museum, networks of love, nostalgia, melancholy and hope circulate which can be best explored through the filter of inter-relational affective dynamics. These objects must compete with more useful, prettier, more cherished possessions and make their way out of stuffed attic spaces into cars, en route to a (possible) re-enchantment at the social history museum.

A walk on the Trail of Wonders

So far, I have contextualised the workings of networked affects within a framework of constructed knowledge at the museum, academic concerns or affectual politics of memory, as in the case of Italy. In this last section I want to explore memory as an organic network of affects which is generated by compassionate interaction and stewardship with the landscape across time. The study of so-called 'group memory', a more manageable scale of investigation than 'collective memory', suggests that the essential feature of the memory of a group is its 'inter-subjectivity'- its network-like nature. The alterity and closeness experienced through the ethnographic encounter with communities in Swat District, Pakistan (Figure 2), make up a compelling, powerful mixture of affective understandings and sensory intensities. The networked affects of local community, visitor, researcher and NGOs is so complex that it may well disrupt and upend traditional modes of scholarship and academic writing. The deep temporality of the final case study constitutes its most poignant node and refracts memory's communicative potential.

Sargah-Sar: The story of a heritage trail in the Kandak Valley, Pakistan

This is the story of a network of hope and reconciliation. The district of Swat in which it takes place has had a fraught history, notably due to the recent Taliban insurgency. Between 2007 and 2009, the Tehreek-i-Taliban Pakistan (TTP) established a reign of terror over the communities of Lower Swat Valley in North-western Pakistan. The Pakistani army intervened swiftly; however, following military operations, 1.7 million valley dwellers were internally displaced (Jones and Fair 2010). The damage caused by the militants was profound, impacting on every area of life in the region. In the process of forming a local Islamist Caliphate, the Taliban enacted an agenda of systematic destruction of much Buddhist Gandharan and pre-Islamic art and architecture.

In fact, Swat has always been on the edge of being something 'other', a borderland. The cultural area of Gandhara is a frontier region, generally considered to be a peripheral zone of the Indo-Pakistan subcontinent. In its heyday, it was regarded as highly influential over the surrounding areas. For a long time Gandhara played 'the role of a crossroads and melting pot of cultures" (Khan 2013: 260). Such syncretic and dialectic processes make frontiers and even any region fluid. In Lower Swat, communities who suffered from the violence of the Taliban regime have learned to make themselves at home in the valleys again after being internally displaced by the Pakistani Army (Qaiser 2009; Jones and Fair 2010).

In the Kandak Valley, Swat, the inborn hospitality of the semi nomadic Gujar dwellers, coupled with a profoundly intimate knowledge of the landscape, makes anyone feel at home during their visit to the Trail of Wonders. National and international activist heritage work in the Kandak and Kotah valleys has enabled the Swat Directorate of

Figure 2: Map of Swat Valley and greater Pakistan (wikicommons).

Archaeology and Museums, and the Government of Khyber-Pakhtunkhwa to establish Swat's first archaeological park- the Trail of Wonders (Biagioli et al. 2016) (Figure 3). The interconnected mesh of affects and ancestral memories making up this extraordinary living heritage landscape leads outsiders to join in the experience of the temporality of the area's stunning heritage holistically. Emotional memories of the Taliban war have become part of cultural networks of emotional performances and enactments that facilitate healing and reconciliation. The abandoned Army checkpoint at the entrance to the Trail of Wonders, a dark blot on a dirt-road framed by cornfields, reminds one that the Military has guarded the security of heritage sites as well as protecting local people and their livelihood from the insurgents' damage. Both heritage sites and people's lives belong in the same network, inseparable and mutually dependent. Further, "Kandak and Kotah Valleys are historic landscapes that are presently lived in. While the historic landscape belongs to the Buddhist community, the present landscape is populated by Muslims which results in a condition of segregation" (Hussain 2016, iii).

The Trail is a way forward, a networked blueprint for hope. Every element and agent has worked together to overcome the trauma of the Taliban insurgency. Swat-specific

Figure 3: Sargah-sar, the Stone with Eyes, in the Trail of Wonders, proudly presented by my co-researcher Ali Shah (photo by the author).

affects are channelled by a meandering track up and down the hills, chasing the past, shaping the present in a holistic network of meanings. The path, or trail, is well maintained and accessible even on slightly muddy conditions. It does not disrupt crops, even when it crosses a small patch of orchard or a cornfield. Along the heritage trail there are no descriptive panels or labels identifying the sites apart from no. 15, the magnificent painted shelter of Sargah-Sar (the face rock in Pashto, the local language, see Figure 3). A sign here (in English) specifies the dating of the site and clarifies its protected status. The two springs signposted along the trail, ancestral and nurturing, restored by the Italian Archaeological Mission, are an example of sustainable heritage intervention. Archaeology, nature and legends blend with local everyday lives along the heritage trail, becoming a seamless part of the everyday tasks and living culture of the Kandak Valley. There is a keen sense of pride and attachment to place by the locals. The political consciousness of the Taliban's damage to their ancestral land feeds back into the Gujars' sense of stewardship for the land in its entirety. The carved and painted shelters and the Gandharan era Buddhist stupas bleed into each other in an implicit timelessness of place-attachment. The local understandings of place disrupt familiar Enlightenment notions of culture and nature.

Without a roadmap to the site or the guidance of local people, I would have missed a few sites. Thankfully the locals who joined our small party were all aware of the precise location of the carvings and paintings along the trail; they could point them out with the utmost confidence, even children. The painted shelters, the paths and donkey's trails, the weather, the homes and the sweet smell of lemongrass are interrelated agents in the affective network that makes the locals feel at home and makes us fall for the timeless spell of the valley. The Gujars nurture a sense of stewardship towards this ancient, ancestral heritage here, which runs alongside a keen awareness of its fragility in a still turbulent area. In Swat, networks of affective belonging have been 'betrayed' by the Taliban's double identity as local and foreign – homegrown and violent. Locals tell me in no uncertain terms that the insurgents might come back, and they may strip the land of yet more treasures.

That said, there is a shared sense of hope. A network of trust in each other's agencies and efforts to restore peace in the area is being formed. Activists continue to provide their services and to educate the young; local elders spread the word of tolerance and respect. The communities are overwhelmingly grateful to their foreign friends, co-researchers and allies, grateful for our compassion, our help, and our shared love for the places that they call home. It is impossible for me to feel as if I have not also entered their affective network, and set out my own emotional stakes in the peace and wellbeing of the people of Swat and their vast and verdant valley.

Conclusions

In and among these networks of affects, legend, hope and dreams, three considerations stand out. One, there can be no sense of place without a keen awareness of the temporality of 'home'; two, communities remember not as one organism, but as a multifaceted network of new, old, first-hand and second-hand recollections; three, storytelling creates its own set of networked memories. The experience of those enmeshed in violent conflict, in World War II Italy and in Swat valley, be it anti-Taliban fighters or members of the valley community, inhabits unique networks of places in memory. Unlike the distribution maps usually accompanying journal publications or monographs, Swat's situated networked histories (or even, stories) transcend representation. Born of conversations and walks with participants, the stories we collected and assembled in Swat Valley evoke emplaced memories riddled with traumatic associations that escape iconography. Far from being linear, dogmatic and clear-cut, people's memories are often the embodiment and re-enactment of events which turned one's world upside down– trauma and tragedies unravelled in often familiar, treasured environs, in one's home village or valley, as in Swat. The voices of Italians and Swat Valley dwellers who recount their tale through embodied everyday enactments and materialities offer a glimpse into the deep complexity of everyday acts of resistance. The agencies in Swat have coalesced in a network of activism and peace-building, resisting violence and fighting to preserve and restore the memories, meanings, imaginations and dreams of local communities. They also remind us of the terror and violence of civil war; voices from the deindustrialised Northeast of England, at the same time, denounce the social disruption brought about by the closure of the coal mines and economic migration to the South and to cities in the UK and abroad. During the Topoi symposium and the conversations that followed, be it in person, by email and in print, three seemingly disconnected nodes in a global network of heritage and history have come together in a moment of reflection. Their affects reached a lecture room in Berlin-Dahlem during the live delivery of an earlier form of this paper. Ultimately, I wanted to anticipate possible tangible *and* intangible impacts of networked affects at heritage sites and in living historical landscapes that cast long shadows onto the present and reach out into a (hopefully less divisive) future.

At the heart of *Mare Nostrum*

Islands and "small world networks" in the central Mediterranean Bronze Age

Helen Dawson

Sicily, Lipari, identity, interaction, world system, network

Introduction

Network graphs can convey complex phenomena very effectively, a factor that has appealed greatly to many archaeologists working on a range of cultural processes. "A picture is worth a thousand words" – as the saying goes. Like with any other model, behind every network graph lies a simplification of reality, the data we use are selected (in the field or in the lab), and – when interpreting the data – a balance needs to be struck between what is "possible" and what is in fact "plausible" (Terrell 2018), as a way to achieve as close as possible an approximation to what actually happened in the past. The way archaeologists choose to convey data, *i.e.* the representation of knowledge – through metaphors, graphs, and images – has an equally profound influence on how others understand what they intend to communicate. A classic example is human migration, which is generally represented graphically in archaeological publications as a series of large arrows on a map. The arrows inevitably convey the idea of large-scale population movement and long-distance directionality, hence migration is generally considered as purposeful and planned. Recent studies, on the other hand, have shown the need to distinguish between migration (usually large scale and long distance) and mobility (which can involve smaller groups, not entire populations, and be local in scale). Such arguments can be explained through text but images are more powerful than words: they stick in the mind for longer (Whitehouse et al. 2006).

When I was a student of European prehistory, in the late 1990s-early 2000s, the prevailing interpretation of interaction in the Bronze Age Mediterranean was that of a

World System (Wallerstein 1974). Under the influence of "Processualism" and systems-thinking in archaeology, World System Theory (WST) focused on economic flows and their directionality, in order to identify areas acting as "cores" and "peripheries". WST found a champion in Andrew Sherratt, who envisioned the Bronze Age Mediterranean as articulated into three broad cultural and geographical zones, a "core" (the Near East), a "periphery" (the Aegean), and a "margin" (the Central Mediterranean and temperate Europe) (Sherratt 1993, 1994, 2011; see also Kristiansen 1998; Kardulias 2009; Kardulias and Hall 2008). Sherratt defined the core as "an urbanised manufacturing zone with bulk transport and state organization"; the periphery as "a raw material supply zone importing manufactured goods"; and the margin as an "area of 'escaped' technologies and long-distance contacts based on directional exchange-cycles" (Sherratt 1993a: 44, fig. 13). While in this scheme interaction was considered as mostly directional, "a pattern of growth from east to west" (Sherratt and Sherratt 1989: 347), Sherratt also saw it as a "creative and dialectical" process between periphery and core, arguing that "peripheries may grow into competing cores (with their own, new peripheries), so that the topology is constantly changing, and creating interstices within which new roles can emerge" (Sherratt and Sherratt 1989: 340).

In this paper, I draw on Sherratt's seminal work (see also Dawson and Nikolakopoulou 2020), approaching Mediterranean Bronze Age interaction through a network perspective. I will focus on the so-called margin, represented here by island and coastal sites in the central Mediterranean. This approach will highlight their role as hubs and gateways for innovation within an emerging "small world" network (Watts and Strogatz 1988). Island and coastal communities in particular, even though located on the so-called "margin", had a definite geographical advantage in terms of being able to initiate and maintain maritime networks. Changes in their livelihood and prosperity did not stem directly from a distant core area, but resulted from changes in the networks themselves, which also affected the core. The advantage of using a network approach is to demonstrate how communities on all sides were affected by interaction and that interaction occurred not only between core, periphery, and margins, but also within them. Furthermore, it shows that communities held various degrees of centrality at different times, clarifying changes in their "topology".

At the heart of *Mare Nostrum*: Networks of interaction

Archaeologists, anthropologists, and historians have long debated the cultural unity of the Mediterranean, emphasising elements of cultural convergence against a background of plurality (Blake and Knapp eds 2005; Braudel 1972; Broodbank 2013; de Pina-Cabral 1989; Horden and Purcell 2000). The distinctive combination of, on the one hand, the topographic fragmentation of the islands and peninsulas, and, on the other hand, the connectivity afforded by the sea has been singled out as a key factor in producing a mosaic of cultural traits, where individual *tesserae* contribute to a degree of unity (Horden and Purcell 2000). In the long term, social interaction resulted in the "Mediterraneanization" (Morris 2003: 30) of local communities, *i.e.* the sharing of cultural traits across increasing distances over time. These studies demonstrate that there are considerable insights to be gained by applying a wide-angle lens and a diachronic perspective on Mediterranean cultures. Nonetheless, as we shall see, far from being a linear process of cultural integration, Mediterraneanisation can be considered the result of the alternating of periods of social cohesion and differentiation (Morris 2003,

	Sicily	Aeolian Islands	Italy	Mainland Greece	Approx. calendar years BC
Early Bronze Age	Castelluccio	Capo Graziano I	Palma Campania	EHIII-MH	2200 – 1700
Middle Bronze Age 1 – 2	Castelluccio Tardo, Rodì Tindari	Capo Graziano II	Proto Appenninico	LHI – II	1700 – 1500
Middle Bronze Age 3	Thapsos	Milazzese	Appenninico	LHIIIA	1500 – 1300
Recent Bronze Age	Pantalica I Nord	Ausonio I	Sub appenninico	LHIIIB	1300 – 1150
Final Bronze Age	Pantalica II - Cassibile	Ausonio II	Proto villanoviano Proto geometrico	LHIIIC	1150 – 900

Table 1: Chronology (adapted from Bietti Sestieri 2015 and Martinelli 2015).

Wallace 2018), a process that is still ongoing and holds great relevance in the present-day context of multiculturalism and globalization (Dawson and Nikolakopoulou 2020; De Angelis ed. 2013; Hodos 2010; Iacono 2019: 4 – 8). In fact, while nowadays political and economic factors have transformed the Mediterranean into a barrier to human migration into Europe, a long-term perspective reveals a completely different role of this "middle sea" in prehistory, as connecting rather than separating, as fostering the creation of cultural identities through interaction. In particular, during the Bronze Age (3rd – 2nd millennium BC), prehistoric communities throughout the Mediterranean were increasingly involved in expanding networks, likely linked to the acquisition of resources but presumably also for socio-cultural purposes (Dawson 2016; Dawson and Nikolakopoulou 2020; Iacono 2019). These networks connected people living in the central Mediterranean with those of the Aegean and the Levant, so that – for the first time – long-distance maritime travel can be documented and its effects studied through archaeological evidence. Seafaring was facilitated by deep-hulled sailing ships at this time, an innovation which effectively warped time and space in terms of travel across the Mediterranean (Broodbank 2006, Broodbank 2013: 416, fig. 8.54). The 14th-century BC Uluburun shipwreck off southwest Turkey is a unique time-capsule of such travelling potential at its height: with its ten tons of copper, one ton of tin, and cargo comprising Near Eastern, Cypriot, Mycenaean, Egyptian, Nubian, central European, central Asian, south Italian and/or Sicilian materials, it demonstrates the sheer scale of Mediterranean inter-regional exchange at this time (Pulak 2001; Bachhuber 2006). But putting aside exceptional finds such as shipwrecks, contact between different geographical areas can be studied systematically from the distribution of exchanged objects and raw materials found at terrestrial sites, which also provide important contextual evidence for their use.

Despite an inherited "Aegeocentric" bias in Mediterranean Bronze Age studies, a more balanced view of interaction has emerged in recent times (*e.g.* Iacono 2013, 2019; Russell 2017; Russell and Knapp 2017; Saltini Semerari 2016; Tanasi and Vella 2015), focusing on local cultural development in the central Mediterranean. Essential to this shift has been the classification of pottery into imports, imitations, and derivatives (Jones et al. 2005; 2014), which has shown the complexity of interaction processes, including differences in the role of external elements in local networks (cf. Blake 2005 and Iacono 2015). Moreover, distinctive features in local domestic and funerary architecture in the central Mediterranean region (specifically proto-urban layouts at sites such as Thapsos in Sicily and Faraglioni on Ustica, as well as tholos tombs at Thapsos) have been shown to have

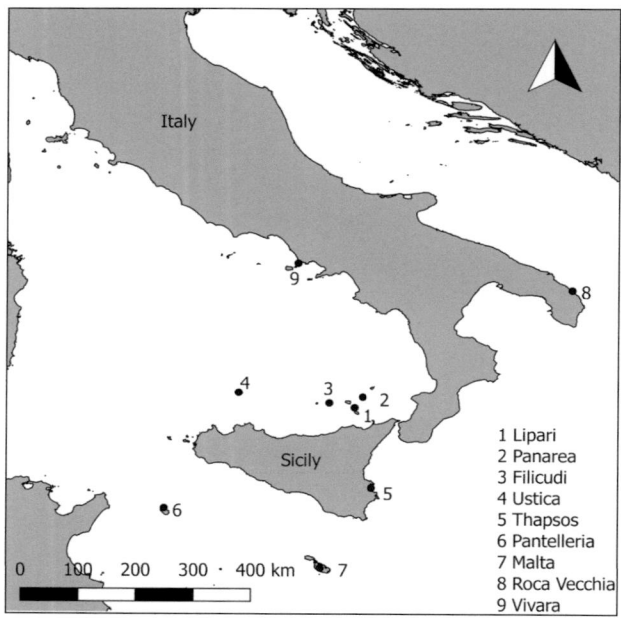

Figure 1: Map of the central Mediterranean with sites mentioned in the text.

local antecedents and development (Leighton 1999; Tusa 2004; Spatafora 2009) rather than stemming directly from foreign influences, which – although undeniable – would have been rather incorporated and adapted to local customs than accepted *tout court*.

It is generally assumed that utilitarian items, raw materials, domestic livestock and their secondary products were exchanged mostly at a local scale during the Neolithic (Leighton 1999; Robb and Farr 2005: 28 – 29), though in some cases covering hundreds of kilometers "down-the-line", as in the case of good quality flint and obsidian. Existing networks may have facilitated the subsequent development of interaction in the Early Bronze Age, with a gradual shift to long-distance movement also of bulk goods (Sherratt and Sherratt 1991). Importantly, contacts between the Aegean and the central Mediterranean began before political centralisation took place at the hands of the Mycenaean palaces (Marazzi 2003). In this respect, it has been pointed out that Early Bronze Age interaction in the central Mediterranean developed as a "decentred network" (Knappett and Nikolakopoulou 2015: 29), where one can follow the connections from various points. Three elements were critical in this process: "mobility, connectivity, and decentring" (Morris 2003: 37).

We begin our exploration of Bronze Age interaction from the island of Lipari. Already an important place in the Neolithic (its obsidian was widely circulated as far as southern France), it declined in the Copper Age with the advent of metal technology, only to resume its central position as a strategic node in the context of expanding maritime networks in the Early Bronze Age (Bernabò Brea 1957). It was during this period (c. 2200 – 1700 BC, corresponding to EH III – MH III), that people from Lipari and the Aeolian Islands engaged in exchange with communities in Southern Italy, as seen from the presence of Aeolian "Capo Graziano" style pottery in contexts dated to the 17th century BC at the site of Punta di Mezzogiorno on the small island of Vivara in the Gulf of Naples, as well as at a

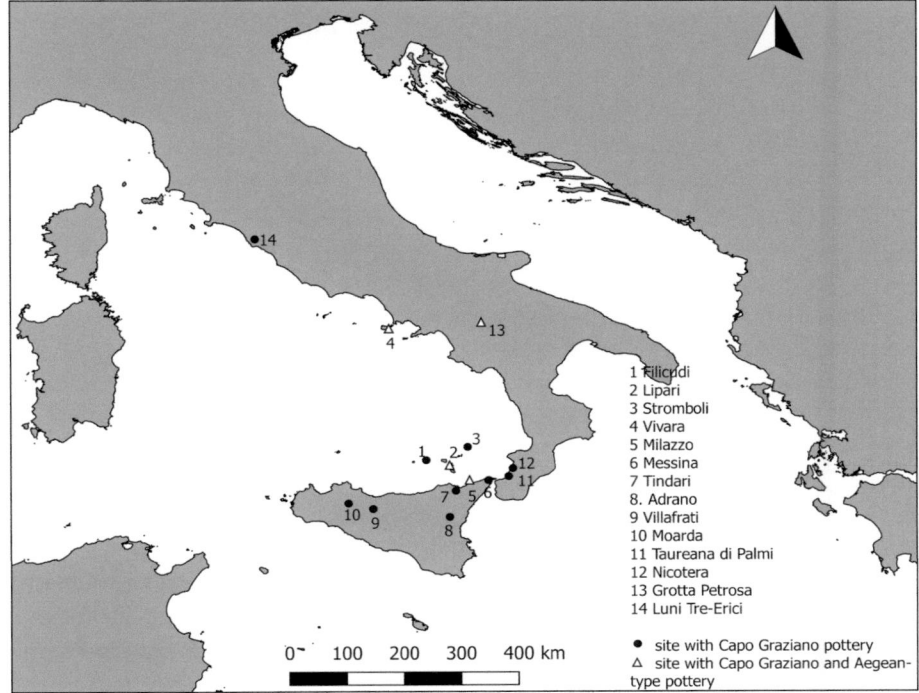

Figure 2: Distribution map of Capo Graziano pottery from the Aeolian Islands in the Central Mediterranean (adapted from Cazzella et al. 1997).

handful of mainland locations.[1] The exact dynamics of these exchanges is unclear: were the islanders transporting the pottery themselves? Nonetheless, the broad distribution of Capo Graziano-style pottery in southern and central Italy is clearly evidence that these small island communities played a role in the budding exchange networks of this time (Figure 2) (Cazzella et al. 1997).

Subsequently, LHI – II Aegean pottery made its first appearance at a few locations which earlier on had Capo Graziano pottery: the island of Vivara (Campania), Grotta Petrosa (Calabria), Milazzo (Sicily), and Lipari itself (Marazzi and Tusa 1994; Rizio 2005: 624; see Fragnoli 2012: 12). It is therefore plausible that communities from the Aeolian Islands, which had already established key maritime routes, actively facilitated an Aegean presence in this region (Cazzella et al. 1997; Copat et al. 2010: 55). Small islands are often considered to be economically marginal, lacking in resources and reliant on the outside world for their livelihood. Marginality, however, is also linked to resourcefulness, *i.e.* the capacity to make the most of what is available, to adapt and innovate (Dawson 2019). In volcanic islands there would have been the need to import clay; nonetheless, more Aeolian pottery

---

1   Capo Graziano-style pottery has been found in Calabria, in the south, at Taureana di Palmi, the necropolis of Nicotera, and Petrosa Cave, and in northern Latium at Luni-Tre-Erici. Ceramics that share similarities with the Capo Graziano style are also reported from the Noglio at Marina di Camerota cave and the Pertosa cave (both in Campania) and S. Angelo III di Cassano Ionio (in Calabria) (see Fragnoli 2012: 57 for a review and primary references).

is found in Sicily than vice-versa, which supports an active role of the islanders in the exchange networks.[2]

Lipari and Vivara were not the only islands already connected at this time: Sicilian sulphur and flint are found on Malta and Maltese "Tarxien Cemetery" pottery has been found in southern Sicily (Palio 2004, in Cazzella and Recchia 2012: 84). Sulphur and alum are also present on the island of Vulcano, in the Aeolian archipelago, and although there is no direct evidence of its exploitation it is unlikely to have gone unnoticed, given that all the nearby islands were settled at this time. Other items being exchanged would have included raw materials, finished products, and foodstuffs. It is plausible that these inter-regional networks expanded pre-existing routes, joining up multiple local networks. It is noteworthy that islanders appear responsible for establishing these networks initially, selecting other islanders (as in the case of Lipari and Vivara) as trading partners.

By the Middle Bronze Age (c. 1700 – 1350 BC, corresponding to LH I – II – IIIA), new players entered the central Mediterranean from the Aegean and Levantine regions. Foreign imports are found in variable quantities at sites in coastal Sicily and Southern Italy, as well as on the Aeolian Islands and the island of Pantelleria (Tanasi 2008; Cazzella and Recchia 2012). Imported items include mostly pottery, from the southern Peloponnese, Crete, and Cyprus, as well as amber and faience beads, fragments of oxhide ingots (found in Sicily at Thapsos, Cannatello, Ognina, and Lipari) and a cylinder seal from Syracuse (Bietti Sestieri 2015: 85). There are fewer sites compared to the EBA, possibly indicating demographic aggregation and increasing socio-cultural centralisation in these areas (Bietti Sestieri 2015: 85).

Aegean pottery is found in exceptionally large quantities at sites identified as "hubs", such as Roca Vecchia in Southern Italy, Lipari in the Aeolian Islands, and Thapsos in south-eastern Sicily. Aegean or Aegean-type pottery is found in both tombs and settlements; with few notable exceptions, it is mostly utilitarian, non-prestige ware, used for local consumption and possibly distribution (Jones et al. 2014; Usai et al. 2009; van Wijngaarden 2002; Vianello 2005). In southern Italy and less commonly in Sicily, Aegean-type pottery was produced locally, imitating the original techniques and styles (Jones et al. 2014). The local production of wheel-made pottery imitating Aegean styles suggests the actual presence of Aegean potters in sites such as Roca, given the rapid adoption of this complex technology. Of particular interest is the imitation of Aegean and Cypriot shapes in the local Thapsos-Milazzese pottery, found along the east coast of Sicily, and of pictorial Mycenaean decorations incised on the local impasto pottery (D'Agata 2000; for Thapsos, see Tusa 1983: 389 – 98; Tanasi 2008: 81; Alberti and Bettelli 2005: 554). In line with post-colonial theory, it is possible to view these innovations not as attempts to emulate the outside world (following an "aegeo-centric" view) but rather as adaptations to the local taste and control or influence over local networks (following an "italic-centric" view) (Vianello 2005; see also Saltini Semerari 2016 and Russell 2017).

At Roca Vecchia, which – as mentioned – may have hosted a sizeable number of Aegean individuals, more than 5000 sherds of Aegean and Aegean-type pottery have been found (mostly dating to LH IIIB2 and early LH IIIC); imports originated mainly in

---

2   Capo Graziano pottery has been found in Sicily along the northern coast facing the Aeolian Islands at nearby Milazzo, Tindari, and Messina, but also in the interior at Adrano, in the Moarda Cave, and at Villafrati (Fragnoli 2012: 57; 118).

the Greek Peloponnese, though pottery was also locally imitated (Guglielmino et al. 2010). The predominance of open shapes – deep bowls and craters – has been linked to wine consumption and feasting between local and non-local individuals (Iacono 2015: 268).

On Lipari, some 300 sherds of Mycenaean pottery (LH I-II and LH IIIA-C) have been found (all the pottery was imported and no imitations were found). The majority is common tableware, distributed throughout the settlements: large quantities were found in a large structure at the Lipari Acropolis, which was possibly associated with feasting and drinking (Van Wijngaarden 2002). There is a lack of storage containers which could indicate interest in the actual pottery rather than its contents (Iacono 2017).

The majority of foreign ceramic finds at Thapsos in SE Sicily comes from the necropolis since the settlement is only partially excavated (Voza 1972, 1973). The repertoire comprises 34 Mycenaean vases and several fragments; three Cypriot vessels, comprising two "Base Ring" and one "White Shaved"; and Maltese "Borg-in-Nadur" material (Tanasi and Vella 2015). These items were linked to high-status individuals, buried in small tholos tombs: they had ornaments in gold, bronze vessels, a few iron items. The high-status burials all had bronze daggers of the Thapsos-Pertosa type. One such sword was found on the Uluburun shipwreck (Vagnetti and Lo Schiavo 1989, 223, fig. 28.2; Pulak 2001, 45 – 6, both in Bachhuber 2006). As different cultures eventually intermixed, distinctions would have been blurred to an extent, as can be inferred from the eclecticism of certain burials in terms of goods (Tanasi and Vella 2015). Tanasi and Vella noted that the burials at Thapsos faced the sea and that this may reflect ideas about connectivity between the local and incoming communities (Tanasi and Vella 2015). We can think of these locations as "gateway communities"[3], providing a cultural passage point (see Iacono infra).

There is evidence for craft specialism in the form of bronze-working activities at Thapsos, where a copper ingot was found. Bronze working activities also took place on the smaller islands, on Pantelleria, Ustica, Lipari, Panarea, and Filicudi. A bronze hoard of 75 kg was found at Lipari Acropolis with fragmentary Thapsos daggers, ingot fragments and shards of bronze bowls. This deposition, the largest known Late Bronze Age hoard in Italy, comprising both Sicilian types, some of Aegean origin, and Italian types, shows that Lipari "controlled remarkable economic resources, which enabled it to acquire raw materials in this period" (Giardino 2000: 100 – 102). These island sites did not rely on locally available raw materials, as was the case with obsidian in the Neolithic, instead it was their location along the trade routes that played to their benefit (Copat et al. 2010: 53).

Other islands, such as Pantelleria, Malta, and Ustica, were not involved in this long-distance network of exchange to the same extent. This does not mean these communities were isolated; on the contrary there is evidence of interaction on a regional scale. On the island of Pantelleria, a community flourished at Mursia, on the western coast of the island. The site has been dated to the Early to Middle Bronze Age (17th-15th centuries BC). Like other contemporary sites, Mursia was located on a naturally defended promontory, with sheer cliffs, while towards the interior it was protected by a monumental stone wall (Cattani et al. 2012). The local pottery style shows links with the EBA Sicilian Rodì-

---

3   Hirth 1978; Branigan (1981) proposes several criteria to define 'gateway' sites from an archaeological perspective, which can be summarised as follows: they occur particularly on the periphery of world systems; at a natural, cultural or economic passage point within a region; they have plentiful imported products and craft specialism/production; there is limited elite hierarchy; and their subsistence is often provided from the outside.

Vallelunga-Boccadifalco culture and with the Aeolian Island culture of Capo Graziano. Aegean-type pottery is lacking, instead the excavators identified matt-painted pottery of possible Levantine type, suggesting that Mursia may have taken part in inter-regional contacts with the eastern Mediterranean, following a maritime route along the North African coast (Ardesia et al. 2006: 72; note though that petrographic analyses have not yet been performed on these sherds). Evidence for bronze-working at the site has also been identified, of particular interest is the production of moulds made from local volcanic stone (Cattani et al. 2012). Peinetti et al. (2015) mention 28 moulds which were probably locally produced to be exported; at least one had traces of metal indicating it had been used locally.

There was apparently no direct contact between Malta and the Aegean and Levantine cultures (Bonanno 2008; Cazzella and Recchia 2012). Malta was rather linked to Sicily, judging from the presence of Maltese "Borg-in-Nadur" pottery at Thapsos (necropolis) and the south-eastern coast of the main island (Tanasi 2015). Similarly, the small island of Ustica, NW of Sicily, was more involved in regional networks and culturally aligned with the Aeolian Islands to the east (Milazzese culture) and to Sicily (Thapsos culture). There is evidence for metallurgy but a lack of foreign imports (despite extensive excavations at the site, a single fragment of Mycenaean pottery has been found so far), which may indicate that Ustica was not involved in inter-regional trade but rather in local and regional networks, possibly bridging Sicily and Sardinia (Spatafora 2009, 2016).

By the late Bronze Age (Italian "Bronzo Recente" 1300 – 1150 BC and "Bronzo Finale" 1150 – 900 BC; corresponding to LH IIIB – C), sites were increasingly being fortified: it is clear that by now maritime connections exposed communities also to potential danger (Broodbank 2013: 431; Tusa 2016: 272). This culminated in a wave of destruction which spared but a few locations at the end of this period. Coastal centres in Sicily, including Thapsos, were abandoned. The destruction was violent on the Aeolian Islands, with evidence of fires (Cazzella and Recchia 2012: 1009; Militello 2005: 593). Following this, only Lipari of the islands continued to be inhabited with a probable influx of population from the Italian mainland (Bernabo Brea 1957; Bietti Sestieri 2010).

The Mycenaean palatial system collapsed too around this time. Even so, there was no obvious interruption in long-distance trade, supporting the idea that it was not a palatial prerogative (the distinct lack of mention of long-distance trade in Linear B tablets lends support to this view – Killen 1985): other agents, possibly refugees, mercenaries, and migrant artisans, may have carried items to Sicily (Eder and Jung 2005: 486; Tanasi 2004, 2005; Vianello 2009). In fact, continued and increasing integration between Aegean and Cypriot elements with Italian and local elements has been noted at Pantalica and contemporary sites in Sicily. Ceramics of Italian tradition were now produced in the Aegean region (with rare direct imports), in reverse to the previous trend (Vianello 2009, Iacono 2012). However, the focus of interaction shifted towards Sardinia and peninsular Italy and Sicily's earlier "internationalism" waned (Bietti Sestieri 1988, 2008: Tusa 1983: 457; Tanasi 2005). Sicily and the Aeolian islands had by this time lost their "role as a connecting factor in the Mediterranean" (Bietti Sestieri 2015: 88). Sardinia gained prominence in the exchange networks that saw Cyprus and the eastern Mediterranean as partners and a decline in Aegean presence (Bietti Sestieri 2015: 90).

A small-world network

The key role of islands and coastal sites for Mediterranean cultural interaction in the Bronze Age should be apparent from the foregoing review and becomes even clearer when approached via network analysis. The data come from existing archaeological publications focusing on selected key sites, both on the islands (the Aeolian Islands, Ustica, and Pantelleria) and along the coast (Thapsos on Sicily and Roca in Southern Italy) (for site locations, see Figure 1).

The map in Figure 3 shows the extent of maritime contacts at the height of interaction. The contacts (listed in detail in the appendix) are shown in a simplified manner both as a matrix (Table 2) and as a network in Figure 4.

The key criterion used for building the networks is straight-forward, namely presence/absence of non-local material culture (especially pottery and metalwork, but also other classes of material mentioned above). Presence/absence was preferred as a criterion to the quantity of each category, in order to take into account potential excavation retrieval bias at the sites. Presence of non-local items was taken as evidence of contact between areas (which in a few cases could be identified more accurately, *e.g.* if supported by petrographic analyses). This simplification does not take into account the possibility of "middlemen"

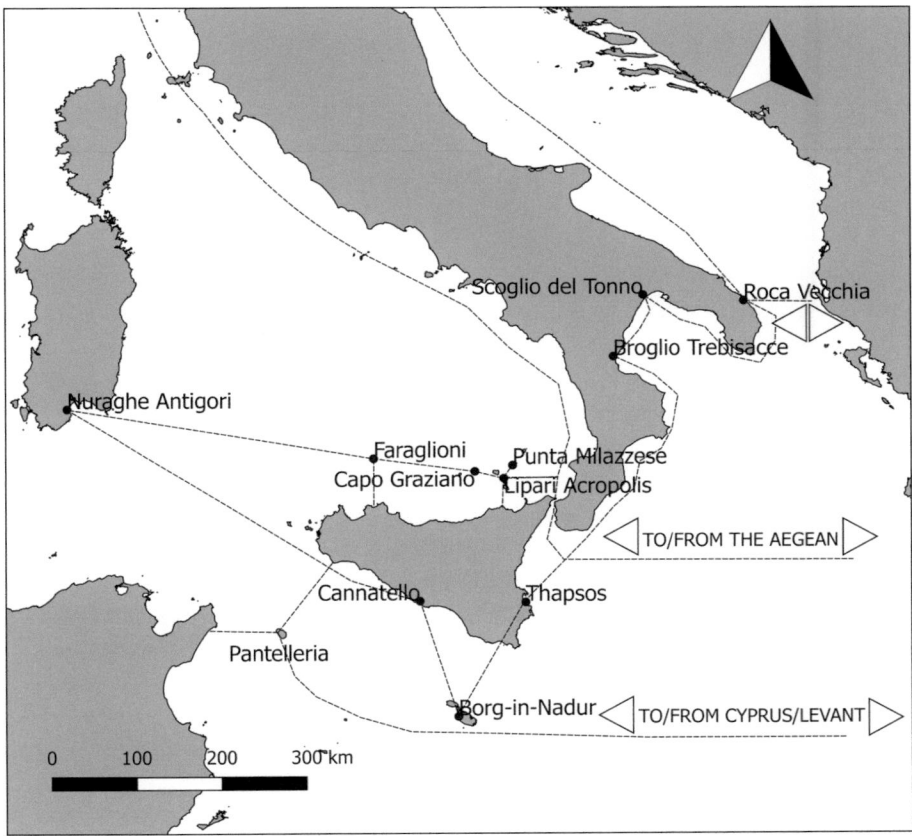

Figure 3: Maritime connections (c. 1500 – 1200 BC) as seen from presence of non-local material culture.

Site	Sicily	Italy	Sardinia	Malta	Aegean	Cyprus/Levant	North Africa
Thapsos (Sicily)	X	X		X	X	X	
Roca Vecchia (Apulia)		X			X		
Acropolis (Lipari)	X	X	X		X		
Faraglioni (Ustica)	X	X	?		X		
Mursia (Pantelleria)	X			X	X	X	?

Table 2: Simplified matrix of contacts on the basis of imported material culture (all types) (c. 1500 – 1200 BC) (see Appendix for details).

(see for example Alberti 2008 for possible Cypriot intermediaries at Thapsos; cf. S. Sherratt 2017: 610), which is likely but hard to assess. If the direction of the exchange is known, this is expressed as a directional link in the network, otherwise the links are undirected.

The database (see Appendix) contains the sites' key characteristics – period, function, presence/absence of desirable local raw materials, presence/absence of foreign resources and objects – and also lists key architectural/burial/ritual features. The network is built using the known distribution of archaeological data, starting with pottery and metalwork and moving on to miscellaneous items. Each dataset could be used conceivably to build a different (but incomplete) network. Here, I have chosen to combine all the data together in one graph to visualize the overall network of interaction. This is of course a rough approximation of cultural interaction as we systematically lack the level of detail necessary (sites are only partially excavated). Moreover, there is an issue of scale, in the sense that the entities being connected are very different (small islands vs. whole regions). Nonetheless, the elements of the network and their role will be described and assessed in light of the archaeological data available.

When viewing interaction at the inter-regional scale, the network resembles a "small world" (Figures 3 – 4) (the resulting graph has the features of a small world network; namely a short average path length and a high clustering coefficient). A "small world" network is a highly clustered network (featuring many hubs rather than a single centre) with short paths between most pairs of nodes (Watts and Strogatz 1988). This is a very common feature of social networks (resulting in the well-known "six degrees of separation" phenomenon) and is considered so efficient it can even be observed in human brain functional systems (Bassett Smith and Bullmore 2006). The "short-cuts" between the nodes in a "small world" ensure connections across the network are maintained even if other nodes no longer exist, making the network more resilient in the long run. Interaction within small world networks can happen very fast; "weak ties" (nodes with fewer connections) create a bridge between clusters (even through occasional contact), providing significant openings for the spread of new ideas (Granovetter 1973). Nodes joining discrete clusters have a higher "betweenness centrality" and function as important "gateways" for innovation (Dawson and Nikolakopoulou 2020). As can be seen in Fig 4, this Bronze Age decentralized network presents several centres or hubs as well as weak links or gateway nodes. In this network, there is no absolute or unique core, periphery or margin, rather nodes display varying degrees of centrality and betweenness.

The "Aeolian Islands", "Thapsos/Sicily" and "Roca/Southern Italy" nodes functioned as hubs (high centrality), with multiple connections at the local, regional, and inter-regional

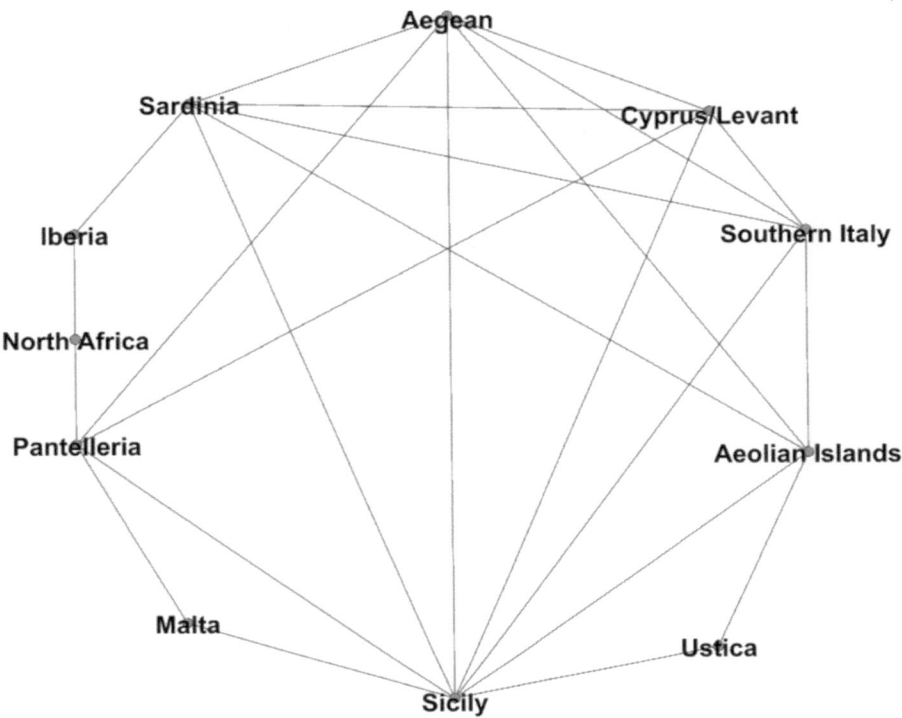

Figure 4: A "small world network" of maritime connections during the Middle to Late Bronze Age (c. 1500 – 1200 BC).

scale, as seen from the high quantities of non-local material culture (especially Aegean-type pottery) retrieved at these sites. Mursia on Pantelleria and Faraglioni on Ustica fit the description of "gateway" sites (given their "betweenness" centrality): although they have strong local and regional links, their inter-regional links are "weak". Their importance lies in the fact that they open up the network to a variety of outside influences, providing a bridge not only towards the east but also to the west (Sardinia, Iberia) and to the south (North Africa). The central Mediterranean was thus also linked to the 'far west', comprising Iberia and North Africa, which were also connected to each other during the Bronze Age (as seen from the presence of African gold, elephant ivory, and ostrich shells in southern Iberia, and Iberian Argaric culture bronze implements and pottery in north-western Africa) (Cunliffe 2017:146 – 8): multiple core-peripheries created a small world network (cf. Malkin 2011; Tartaron 2018; and Knappett 2017, who also identify small world network dynamics in the context of Bronze and Iron Age Aegean interaction).

Conclusions

Viewing Bronze Age interaction as a Small World network underscores the key role of island and coastal sites, which is absent from a rigid core-periphery perspective. If we view these sites as open contact zones and gateway communities, their role within this Small World network can be considered to be "marginal" not because they were geographically isolated from the core, but in the sense that they lay on the edge of different cultural areas, taking advantage of their "in-betweenness" (Dawson 2019). As communities established social connections, they were able to overcome the geographical restrictions imposed by insularity. In this respect, insularity is not fixed in time, or a synonym of isolation, it rather comprises the alternating phases of centrality and marginality that islanders tend to experience over the longue durée. These shifts had an effect on communities and their group identities, often leading to distinct cultural phenomena on the islands. This process of "identification through interaction" (Dawson 2020) was not the result of one-sided acculturation from a core but rather of multiple-sided cultural interaction. As such, it is most evident at times of increased interaction in the Mediterranean, such as was the Bronze Age. Local networks were the essential building block for the establishment of long-distance connections across the Mediterranean (cf. S. Sherratt 2017: 602). The small island- and coastal sites of the central Mediterranean were integral to the creation of the networks, as early as the Neolithic. Insularity and maritime access along the coast are geographical features which enabled social interaction on an unprecedented scale. At the same time, social interaction overcame geographical limitations in the case of small islands, such as lack of resources. Centrality and marginality are to be considered dynamic, social constructs, not as fixed entities. Hence, a network perspective, with its bottom-up approach, shows us the building blocks of this dynamic process as we begin to study cultural phenomena also from the perspective of in-between or interstitial spaces (cf. Sherratt 2017: 615).

The Middle to Late Bronze Age (c. 1500 – 1200 BC) saw the earliest establishment of trans-Mediterranean contacts. At this time, thanks to a "proliferation of networks" (Sherratt 2017: 608), the Mediterranean achieved the configuration of a *Mare Nostrum*, an interconnected space facilitating cultural integration as opposed to one-sided acculturation. The contacts in effect created the space, with networked dimensions. This is not to deny directionality or that external influences existed but rather to emphasise the local element in this process and that all sides were involved. Cultural interaction also resulted in tension: over time, the importance of the original hubs and gateways decreased and a few were abandoned and even destroyed by the Final Bronze Age. Nonetheless, even without those nodes, inter-regional connections continued to exist because of the resilient structure of the small world network, only to be further transformed as new players entered the scene at the dawn of the Iron Age.

Appendix

SITE	THAPSOS
Location	Sicily
Function	Settlement and tombs
Period of occupation	14th – 12th c. BC
Local chronology	MBA, RBA, FBA
Aegean Bronze Age chronology	LHIII A1 – LHIIIC
Local raw materials	clay
Imported raw materials	copper, tin/bronze
Regional imports	Maltese Borg-in-Nadur pottery, Apennine pottery (mainland Italy)
Archaeometric analysis (from Jones et al. 2014)	8 Mycenaean probably imported from the Peloponnese (from the burials)
Quantity of Aegean and Italo-Mycenaean pottery (Jones et al. 2014)	few fragments from the settlement (still unpublished, no analysis); from the burials: 34 Mycenaean vases and several fragments
Cypriot imports	2 Base Ring II Ware and 1 White Shaved Ware (from the burials) (no analysis)
Mycenaean clay figurines	No
Ivory objects	n/a*
Seal stones	n/a*
Vitreous material (*e.g.* beads)	Yes
Oxhide ingots	Yes
Metalwork (raw material)	Yes
Metal objects	bronze hemispherical bowl
Metalwork features (molds, casts, waste, etc)	Yes
Fortification	Yes
Planned settlement	Yes
Tholos-like tombs or monumental structures	Yes (tholos burials)
System of writing/recording	No
Local imitations of foreign pottery	Yes
Selected bibliography*	La Rosa (2000: 135); La Rosa (2004: 14), Lo Schiavo (2006: 1325 – 8); Voza 1972, 1973

*Site is only partly published

SITE	MURSIA
Location	Pantelleria
Function	Settlement and tombs
Period of occupation	17th – 16th c. BC
Local chronology	EBA, MBA
Aegean Bronze Age chronology	MHIII – LHIII
Local raw materials	obsidian
Imported raw materials	clay, red ochre, copper, tin/bronze
Regional imports	Sicilian pottery, casting molds made from non-local sandstone, possibly Maltese and Aeolian pottery (stylistic similarities, no analysis)
Archaeometric analysis (from Jones et al. 2014)	None (but see Secondo et al. 2011)
Quantity of Aegean and Italo-Mycenaean pottery (Jones et al. 2014)	n/a
Cypriot imports	Cypriot or Levantine bichrome pot (no analysis)
Mycenaean clay figurines	No
Ivory objects	bracelets, hippo tusk
Seal stones	No
Vitreous material (*e.g.* beads)	Yes
Oxhide ingots	No
Metalwork (raw material)	Yes
Metal objects	Yes (awls, hooks, bracelets, pendant, foil, bead fragments, etc)
Metalwork features (molds, casts, waste, etc)	molds, metallic filaments, smelting drop
Fortification	Yes
Planned settlement	Yes
Tholos-like tombs or monumental structures	Yes (Sesi)
System of writing/recording	potter's marks, tokens
Local imitations of foreign pottery	n/a
Selected bibliography	Ardesia et al. 2006; Cattani et al. 2012

SITE	FARAGLIONI
Location	Ustica
Function	Settlement
Period of occupation	15th – 13th c. BC
Local chronology	MBA, RBA?
Aegean Bronze Age chronology	LHIII B – C
Local raw materials	Basalts
Imported raw materials	clay, obsidian
Regional imports	Apennine ware (mainland Italy), Aeolian pottery, Sardinian pottery?
Archaeometric analysis (from Jones et al. 2014)	1 plain Italo-Mycenaean (uncertain)
Quantity of Aegean and Italo-Mycenaean pottery (Jones et al. 2014)	2 fragments (stirrup jar)
Cypriot imports	No
Mycenaean clay figurines	No
Ivory objects	No
Seal stones	No
Vitreous material (*e.g.* beads)	Yes
Oxhide ingots	No
Metalwork (raw material)	Yes
Metal objects	Yes
Metalwork features (molds, casts, waste, etc)	mold for flat axes
Fortification	Yes
Planned settlement	Yes
Tholos-like tombs or monumental structures	No
System of writing/recording	potter's marks, tokens
Local imitations of foreign pottery	No
Selected bibliography	Mannino 1992; Spatafora 2016

SITE	ROCA VECCHIA
Location	Italy
Function	Settlement and tombs
Period of occupation	16th – 8th c. BC
Local chronology	MBA, RBA, FBA, IA
Aegean Bronze Age chronology	LMIIIA – LMIIIB, LH II – Sub-mycenaean
Local raw materials	murex shell
Imported raw materials	copper, tin/bronze, amber, gold
Regional imports	dolia
Archaeometric analysis (from Jones et al. 2014)	1 matt-painted, 1 burnished, 2 Mynian, 18 Mycenaean probably Peloponnese, Central Greece and west Crete, 17 Italo-Mycenaean, 4 Grey, 4 dolia, 2 basins, 3 Protogeometric, 11 impasto, 2 various
Quantity of Aegean and Italo-Mycenaean pottery (Jones et al. 2014)	ca. 2000 fragments, 8 MH: minian, matt-painted and fine orange burnished; Mycenaean: 90% Lustrous Decorated
Cypriot imports	No
Mycenaean clay figurines	No
Ivory objects	Minoan ivory objects
Seal stones	Yes
Vitreous material (*e.g.* beads)	Yes
Oxhide ingots	No
Metalwork (raw material)	Yes
Metal objects	two hoards, with gold and bronze objects, including a sword of Aegean type (Middle Helladic – sub-Mycenaean), Cypriot-type tripod and knives? Aegean, Balkans, northern Italian types
Metalwork features (molds, casts, waste, etc)	Yes
Fortification	Yes
Planned settlement	Yes
Tholos-like tombs or monumental structures	No
System of writing/recording	No
Local imitations of foreign pottery	Yes
Selected bibliography	Guglielmino 2003, 2005

SITE	ACROPOLIS
Location	Lipari
Function	Settlement
Period of occupation	56th – 10th c. BC
Local chronology	Neolithic, Eneolithic, EBA, MBA, RBA, FBA
Aegean Bronze Age chronology	LH I – II, LHIIIA – C
Local raw materials	obsidian
Imported raw materials	copper, tin/bronze, flint and clay (from Sicily)
Regional imports	Sicily (Thapsos pottery), Apennine pottery (mainland Italy), 5 Nuragic-type fragments imported from Sardinia
Archaeometric analysis (from Jones et al. 2014)	9 Mycenaean probably imported from the Peloponnese, 1 pithos uncertain, 5 Nuragic-type fragments imported from Sardinia
Quantity of Aegean and Italo-Mycenaean pottery (Jones et al. 2014)	>300 fragments
Cypriot imports	No
Mycenaean clay figurines	Yes
Ivory objects	bone or ivory comb
Seal stones	Yes
Vitreous material (*e.g.* beads)	Yes
Oxhide ingots	Yes
Metalwork (raw material)	Yes
Metal objects	hoard containing Italian mainland axes, Peschiera and Thapsos swords and daggers, fragments of metal sheet vessels
Metalwork features (molds, casts, waste, etc)	Yes
Fortification	Yes
Planned settlement	Yes
Tholos-like tombs or monumental structures	San Calogero Tholos
System of writing/recording	potter's marks, tokens
Local imitations of foreign pottery	No
Selected bibliography	Bernabò Brea and Cavalier 1968, 1980.

Marx, networks and the social logic of interaction

Francesco Iacono

Networks, Marxist theory, culture contact, mode of interaction, social conflict

The network hype and why networks are not enough

In the last two decades or so, gradually but steadily, the concept of network has acquired considerable importance, mainly as a metaphor through which to filter our understanding of society. Cultural theorists and specialists in media studies have been at the forefront of this development, often borrowing keywords from the work of social physics and transforming them into loose metaphors (i.e. Barabási, 2002; Castells, 1996; Prey, 2012). The affirmation of such a trend, though, has not occurred without criticism. Boltanski and Chiapello (2005), for instance, have stigmatised the tendency to apply the logic of networks to the analysis of contemporary social phenomena. In their view this is a very recent development that flattens dynamics of exploitation in a dualistic dichotomy of inclusion vs. exclusion and that projects a negative 'halo' on those who are excluded. Without endorsing the efficacy and versatility of the inclusion/exclusion paradigm *tout-court*, it is certain that, although deficient, this paradigm is not limited to capitalism and the modern 'internet' society. Indeed, as recognised long ago by anthropologists (*e.g.* Barth 1969), the inclusion/exclusion dynamics is critical to many pre-modern contexts *e.g.* in various forms of membership, identity formation, and ethnicity. However, the problem runs deeper and underlies the basic question of whether focusing on inclusion/exclusion is enough; that is, if the network metaphor has completely cancelled the need for more traditional theoretical tools in order to make sense of society and its multiple facets. Have networks superseded "class"?

My short answer to this question is no. Despite the fact that much has changed and new constructs can, and indeed have been, adopted, in my view, the notion of class (in the sense specified below) still represents an unavoidable analytical tool (Wright 2000). The network as a concept captures only some elements of interaction, but a more in-depth approach is required in order to understand social dynamics in pre-modern and modern contexts alike. Some of the earliest adopters of networks in the social sciences, *i.e.*

sociologists of the Social Network Analysis (Scott 2010; Wasserman 1994), were well aware of the existing linkage with other forms of social theory, and considered Marx's work as an important building block of their theoretical development (Emirbayer 1997; White 2008). In this paper I will try to build on this engagement, expanding on connections with existing branches of social theory. I will focus specifically on Marxism and related strands of radical social theory because this, in all its multiform versions, has been particularly effective in highlighting the importance of social conflict as a trigger of social change. Somewhat unusually given this starting point, my focus will be on inter-societal relations, a domain that has often been neglected in traditional explanations of social dynamics but that is crucial if we are to understand phenomena in all their complexity. In particular, the proposal that will be presented here tries to 'upgrade' some of the concepts of Marxist social theory with a specific attention to pre-modern societies (both archaeologically, historically and ethnographically documented), integrating them with networks and highlighting the advantages of doing so.

Marx revisited

For Marxism every relation is an internal one, meaning that everything that matters takes place within a society and external aspects are less important (Ollman 2003). This is a somewhat limited view in that we cannot ignore the powerful distinctions brought on by space between societies, in defining us vs. them. Therefore, it will be necessary to move from an analysis of society at-large to an analysis of individual societies (and their relations). This does not mean falling back to common-sense categories such as modern 'national' societies (Friedman 2008). Rather, the total of "Society" is the articulation of similar relationships functioning at various scales. Society at-large is just the agglomeration of a complex set of smaller units.

Before moving to the description of the emendation of classical Marxist theory that I will adopt, it will be necessary to clarify a pervasive conceptual misunderstanding relating to the notion of production in Marx, which has been heavily criticised over the last few decades (Baudrillard 1975; Benton 1989; Friedman 1974; Rowlands and Gledhill 1998). As we will see, Marx's notion of "production" was in fact much more nuanced than what has been acknowledged by some of his critics, encompassing both production and consumption and their relations with ecosystems (Foster 2000; Gregory 1982; Meillassoux 1975).

Directly connected to this consideration is the notion of "capital" that I will adopt. Following a prolific tradition of studies in sociology and anthropology (Bourdieu 1986; Godelier 1999; Graeber 2001; Gregory 1982; Mauss 1966), the notion of capital adopted here escapes the economic-oriented underpinnings often entailed by the common-sense use of the word. Rather, in pre-modern settings, capital is congealed human labour in its explicit (actual work, products) and implicit (obligations ratified through a variety of social practices and sanctions) forms. As a result, what is here defined as capital encompasses a variety of aspects "expendable" in the arena of social interactions including:

"food, women [*and men*, I might add], children, possessions, charms, land, labour, services, religious offices, rank – everything is stuff to be given away and repaid. In perpetual interchange of what we may call spiritual matter, comprising men and things, these elements pass and repass between clans and individuals, ranks, sexes and generations." (Mauss 1966: 10 – 12).

In other words, the definition of capital adopted here encompasses value in its purest form, notwithstanding its social manifestation (for a similar but not identical point of view in the Marxist tradition see Bourdieu 1986; Luxemburg 2003). Phrased in such a way, this definition may appear to some extent static, but this objection does not consider the dynamic nature of societies themselves. As the conditions of material production and social transactions mutate within and across societies (see below), so does the nature of the social relations and values involved.

Means, Relations and Modes of Production

The conceptual clarifications introduced in the previous section have important consequences for the theory presented here, leading to a reassessment of some of the basic categories of Marxism. I will focus on two important aspects of Marxist theory, "Means of Production" and "Relations of Production" and propose a framework for studying inter-societal dynamics, in terms of hegemonic relations between groups or classes, through an appreciation of their "Means of Interaction" and "Relations of Interaction".

"Means of Production", as is well known, have been traditionally considered the tools through which production occurs (occasionally including also human qualities directly affecting production: *e.g.* skills and muscle force, see Cohen 2000: 33, 44), but this can be limiting and a broader interpretation can be proposed. Instruments of labour also include immaterial aspects that is 'all the objective conditions necessary for carrying on the labour process' (Marx 1976: 286; see also Hebblewhite 2012). Such an interpretation is in line with a general trend in Marxist theory, essentially started by western Marxism (Althusser 1969; Gramsci 1971; Lukács 1971) and generally aimed at overcoming the rigid division between structure (or economic base) and superstructure of 'vulgar materialism' (see Lukács 1971). The broad interpretation of Means of Production adopted here might spur some confusion with another category critical in Marx's theory of history to which the immaterial side was traditionally mostly confined, and this is the notion of "Relations of Production". These are just normal relationships (among many others present in the social field) but they acquire a determining role in that they come to control the access to the Means of Production. The difference between the two concepts can be evinced from the continuation of the same passage from the first volume of the Capital, where it is specified that "… [Means of Production] do not enter directly into the [labour] process, but without them it is either impossible for it to take place, or possible only to a partial extent. […] Instruments of this kind, which have already been mediated through past labour, include workshops, canals, roads, etc." (Marx 1976: 286 – 7). On the contrary Relations of Production involve social actors, *i.e.* entities that are not only *media* through which the process of social reproduction happens, but also actively partake in it.

Despite their complexity, Relations of Production can be analytically broken down to a relationship between two groups or, to use a much neglected term, "classes" (see Carrier and Kalb 2015): one made of people chiefly producing surplus and one chiefly appropriating the surplus produced. Such a consideration is universally accepted neither in Marxism nor in Anthropology. And yet more or less subtle forms of exploitation are possible in any social configuration, even in kin-ordered societies (e.g. Wolf 2010: 91). The confrontation between unequal groups or classes, although expressed in different ways, will always entail three potential results: one or the other class will be hegemonic or the two will reach a more or less precarious equilibrium.

A second pivotal concept within Marx's theory of history is that of "Modes of Production". These are substantially different from typologies used by social evolutionism (*e.g.* Service 1962) because they are inherently dynamic and do not correspond necessarily to specific political forms (Friedman 2008). Given our focus, in the present context Mode of Production rather than representing ideal types, actually stands for their embodiment in specific social/territorial units (lineages, communities, villages, cities, and so on). We can therefore argue that each of these social units will have a slightly different configuration and hence a variation in the way Relations of Production operate, and thus, differences in their Mode of Production.

Towards a non-neutral notion of interaction

The emendation proposed so far relates to the classical domain of action of Marxist social theory. It will be necessary now to move to the inter-societal domain. In this, we are not much helped by Marx and Engels themselves, whose interest was primarily in individual entities, abstracted to a considerable degree. This is not to say that Marx and Engels did not discuss communication, exchanges and all the social implications of these aspects. One of the most interesting commentaries on Marxist notions of interaction are offered by De La Haye, an early media theorist who collected some of the most interesting passages on this topic from the work of Marx and Engels (De La Haye et al. 1980). The object of his discourse is, naturally enough, communication and the means through which it occurs even though what it actually deals with (given also the historical *milieu* in which the original sources were written) can be put under the label of inter-societal interaction without stretching the interpretation too much. According to De La Haye, communication/interaction is not just part of the productive forces but rather can be considered an integral part of Relations of Production (for a similar point see also Williams 1977; Hebblewhite 2012). Communication networks were not static constructs but instead 'accompanied societies' development at all times, changing their material base and mode of operation in function of the levels attained by the mode of production' (De La Haye et al. 1980: 30). At the same time, a fundamental ambiguity is noted for means of communication and 'their double role as elements of the productive forces, and as the social relations of production, factors in the formation of a new social personality, that is new sensibilities, new interests, new ways of relating to the world etc.' (De La Haye et al. 1980: 29).

These are important insights, although if we are to fully accomplish the shift from the analysis of society at-large to that of concrete societies in their mutual relations, it will be necessary to rephrase the very categories previously described, "fractally" extending them to the *terra incognita* (in classic Marxist terms) of the inter-societal domain. Such a complex task has been attempted, among others, by World-System theorists, anthropologists and historians of the *longue-durée*, who noting the inescapable necessity for a supra-local unit of analysis, have been all too aware of the difficulties introduced by dealing with the articulation of different components (Arrighi 1994; Friedman 2008; Wallerstein 1974; Wolpe 1980). As is well known, the need for supra-local units of analysis lead World-System Analysis (following "Dependency theory") to the introduction of two new categories of analysis, *i.e.* core and periphery. The discussion here presented is not incompatible with this solution. Still, in contrast to World-System Analysis, the focus here is not on the global scale, but rather on the very mechanics of how external relations influence individual social realities involved in interaction, as well as how this outcome is further modified by the logic of multiple connections and networks.

A first consideration with regard to an inter-societal Marxist approach is that actually interaction is (particularly prior to the advent of modern communication) often confined to discrete real-world encounters rarely enacted by whole societies but normally by segments of them. Such encounters have been the object of enquiry of many post-colonial theorists and the influence of this discussion has also resonated within a broad disciplinary field including also archaeology (Cornell and Fahlander 2007; Van Dommelen and Rowlands 2012). As far as our discussion is concerned, the main takeaway point is that encounters are never neutral but always encompass a power imbalance.

This is because not all groups of people are equally able to access the means through which interaction happens. Like for Means of Production, these means, which are here defined as Means of Interaction, can be either material, as for instance a cart or a donkey, or a ship that is equipped and used to move people and/or goods from one place to another, and/or social, as is, for example, the acknowledgement of the membership of a clan or family within a small circle of international elite exchange (*i.e.* the case of the gift exchange attested between sovereigns in the Amarna Letters in the Eastern Mediterranean, or the Kula Ring in the Trobriand Islands; see Leach and Leach 1983; Liverani 2002; Moran 1992). The definition of Means of Interaction here proposed falls in part within that of Means of Production whilst in part coincides with what Marx rather dismissively defined as "circulation costs" (Marx 1992: 207-229). These were something "that arise simply from a change in form of the commodity [that] cannot add any value to it" (Marx 1992: 226-227). While this is undoubtedly true from the vantage point of the individual entity, if we put at the centre the relationship between actors, this domain becomes the one that has the largest effect on the encounter of which interaction is made of. The surplus invested in the Means of Interaction becomes the main factor on which processes of class differentiation and exploitation are based at the supra-local level.

On this basis, it is possible to introduce a further concept, *i.e.* that of Modes of Interaction, constituted by the intersection in space of different Modes of Production. As with Relations of Production, the different positioning of groups with respect to the Relations of Interaction can create a class division that transgresses the boundaries of individual societies. The interests of these two new classes need not be the same as those created by Relations of Production. As a consequence, a contradiction emerges between these two sets of interests, namely those referring to internal and external (*i.e.* inter-societal) classes. The effects of interaction on the social structure of different entities involved will vary widely, depending basically on the results of the process of negotiation between these interests. Indeed, when in one society the group (or class) which interacts and controls the Means of Interaction does not correspond to that controlling the Means of Production, and interaction is able to produce a considerable amount of capital, then this may result in a shift of the internal power balance (that is, a change in internal Relations of Production). On the contrary, when Relations of Interaction favour the same class dominant in Relations of Production, it is possible to suggest that the result will be a reinforcement of the existing order.

Groups with a relatively better position in Relations of Interaction (*i.e.* hegemonic) are in a privileged position as controlling the means through which interaction takes place; they can interrupt the connection channel or divert it towards another destination. On the contrary, those who are non-hegemonic in Relations of Interaction are left only with the possibility to "accept" or "decline" connections and have limited possibilities to influence their course. This is not to say that they lack the means to "produce" social value via "interaction", but rather that such production will be by and large at least potentially controlled by hegemonic actors.

The role of hegemony and material culture

I have characterised the ways in which class relationships (both within the same Mode of Production and in the Mode of Interaction) are negotiated as hegemony, adopting a concept central to the work of Antonio Gramsci (Cospito 2004; Gramsci 1971); the use of this notion, however, deserves a further clarification that I will try to offer here.

Hegemony as a concept is not new to archaeology and anthropology (see Crehan 2002). Hegemony mediates class relationships through a combination of coercion and consent and Gramsci identifies its realm of action in civil society, within the boundaries of the modern bourgeoisie state (Cospito 2004). The less power roles are formalised, the more coercion/force, impression, charm and subjugation become important. The range of action of these factors is all subsumed within the boundaries of lived social encounters (Cornell and Fahlander 2007; Faier and Rofel 2014), the "third space" (Bhabha 1994) in which the balance of hegemony is negotiated, and can hinge upon sentiments as different as fear, suggestion, expectation, sense of power/prostration. The critical nature of the social encounter has been highlighted in the work of many scholars. Such domain is equally relevant at the level of connections between different societies and Gramsci explicitly acknowledged the validity of the use of hegemony at different geographical and spatial scales (Arrighi 1994: 27 – 30; Cospito 2004; Cox 1983). We can therefore speak of hegemony in Relations of Production and in Relations of Interaction. In her *Ulysses' Sails*, Mary Helms (1988) highlighted some of the features that can be considered critical in influencing hegemonic balance as resulting from confrontation between individuals (but the same logic applies for groups of people) coming from different contexts (classes within Modes of Interaction), chiefly in small-scale, premodern societies. These qualities (again showed through performance of some sort) were primarily the knowledge of distant lands and the enchanting aura of mystical *savoir-faire* of travelling, as an action, particularly in the eyes of those excluded from it (for various examples see Helms 1988: 131 – 148; Sahlins 1995: 175-177). Such properties contribute considerably to the balance of what we have defined as Relations of Interaction. The notion of performance I have advocated here is an extremely broad one, in which material culture has a crucial role, helping to define the relative hegemony of one class with respect to another. Clothes, language, equipment, body ornamentation, goods/gifts and means of transportation are all facets of the same representation.

Material culture offers clues regarding the nature of the Relations of Interaction between entities that interact. Indeed, when a group or a class (according to our terminology) is relatively hegemonic in Relations of Interaction, then some of its cultural traits will be appropriated by the group that is non-hegemonic within the context of the encounter. This is because the adoption of such traits signals to the rest of society that *does not* take part in interaction, the closeness of local partners (often corresponding with local elites) with their powerful associates (Helms 1988: 148 – 9). Quite predictably, if external relationships are critical to the maintenance of a dominant position in Relations of Production, then it is possible to argue that, lacking other forms of restriction, these exogenous cultural traits will be appropriated in processes of competition for political and/or social power, ultimately spreading and becoming more and more popular.

Objects bearing these exogenous traits (sometimes termed "preciocities" in the jargon of World System Theory) are *cultural diacritics* expressing what has been defined as *salient affiliation* between the two different interacting groups (Helms 1988: 111 – 130; Schortman 1989). From this, it can be argued that the larger the quantity and the range of material cultural features and/or items appropriated from one area to the other, the stronger is the position of the society which is emulated in Relations of Interaction. This process of 'influence' does not limit itself to material culture but can potentially mediate deep processes of social emulation involving fairly specific social practices such as language or political organisation (*e.g.* Renfrew 1999). Of course, these social practices and the social relations entailed by them (with the related balance of hegemony) will not produce relevant effects, remaining so to speak 'inactive', as long as the right conditions in internal Relations of Production are absent (*i.e.* a local chief, normally, will not build for himself a royal palace as long as its role is not institutionalised in a way similar to that of a king, although forms of mystification are also possible). If these comparable conditions *do* emerge, then it is likely that these practices will become more socially significant, although, of course, they will not produce identical results, with the acquired cultural traits being transformed and acquiring different meanings in any new context.

Networks and the weight of space

Moving from interaction between two actors to whole networks changes the model considerably. Such changes follow theoretical concerns which are not entirely new and that have already been explored by Social Network Analysts. Graph Theory (*i.e.* the branch of mathematics used by Social Network analysts), nevertheless, represents only a tool whose utility is given by its overall theoretical framework. It will be therefore necessary to go back to the notions previously introduced to try to see how they relate to this new level of analysis.

When interaction occurs among many actors, that is, many groups coming from several different societies, the relative position and topological relations between entities involved in interaction acquire noteworthy importance. As previously suggested by De La Haye et al. (1980: 30) networks actually have the power to change the "material base and mode of operation" of societies and hence their Mode of Production. The relative weakness of class-groups in Relations of Interaction is strongly countered if they are involved in a large number of relations. The absolute number of multiple links improves the position of a society in Relations of Interaction, as it allows the introduction of resources (*i.e.* capital) from contact with several other class-groups from different communities. This, in turn, modifies internal Relations of Production and the amount of capital available to be invested for Means of Interaction. Such dynamics is of course at work only as long as the connections are not transformed into a complete subjugation, as in this case what we define Relations of Interaction will effectively become internal Relations of Production of the occupier. Besides having a high number of interactions in absolute terms, the other element that is able to change Relations of Interaction is a strategic position (spatial, political or social) in relation to some extremely valued and restricted resource/s. Entities that are placed in these favourable positions can therefore enjoy a considerable advantage in transactions with other Modes of Productions and very often will manage to increase their level of capital accumulation and hence the amount of resources available for improving their Means of Interaction. In other words, having many different connections automatically improves the possibility of becoming hegemonic in at least some of the relationships involved.

Both hypotheses echo two specific notions of centrality used in Social Network Analysis and these are Degree centrality and Betweenness (Borgatti and Everett 2006; Freeman 1979). These concepts take as a starting point the network as a mathematical abstraction formed by nodes connected to one another through edges. Degree centrality, from a purely operational point of view, is constituted by the absolute count of edges uniting one node with other nodes. According to Freeman "as the process of communication goes on in a social network, a person who is in a position that permits direct contact with many others should begin to see himself and be seen by those others as a major channel of information" (Freeman 1979: 219 – 220) and this point remains valid also at the level of interacting communities. It is only necessary to replace the term 'person' with 'community' or 'class-group' and to add to 'information' also 'capital', in order to make the concept of Degree Centrality useful to this discussion. Betweenness, instead, can be defined as "the frequency with which a point falls between pairs of other points on the shortest or geodesic paths connecting them" (Freeman 1979: 221). Betweenness is based on a different rationale from Degree Centrality as it basically measures the possibility of control that one node has with respect to overall network communication. Again, it is sufficient here to use "society" or "Mode of Production" instead of "point" (here equivalent to "node") to appreciate how this measure is potentially able to disclose the working of Relations of Interaction.

The critical role of networks in modifying what we have termed as hegemony in Relations of Interaction can be synthesised even more tautly following Network Exchange Theorists (Markovsky et al. 1993; Walker et al, 2000). According to this discipline in a triad of interacting nodes a-b-c a structural advantage is gained by the node b where it has the ability to enter in a relationship with both a and c whilst both nodes need necessarily to pass through b. Replacing nodes with communities or even societies, allows us to make sense of one of the most basic configurations of interaction with multiple actors. This logic is also what dominates the behaviour of the "networker", described by Boltanski and Chiapello (2005) as the great man of the "connexionist" world, whose power is based on the amount of links he manages to establish. The main difference between the proposal advanced here and Network Exchange Theory resides in the fact that the latter has its foundations in a universalisation of the profit-seeking "*homo economicus*", which is not tenable for premodern contexts typical of the anthropological discourse (Graeber 2001). The same applies to the networker evoked by Boltanski and Chiapello (2005), a typification ultimately deriving from the managerial-sociological literature of the 1990s. An important distinction to this extent is that Boltanski and Chiapello do not just describe the role of the networker but also try to highlight how the process of exploitation in the connexionist world may look like. In their view, this is identified in the relationship between mobile and immobile actors where mobility is associated with power and immobility with being exploited. The power of mobile actors is grounded in the weakness of the non-mobile ones. While it is possible to agree on this recurrent association (mobility = strength; immobility = weakness; as suggested also by Helms, 1988) contrasting these two elements is not enough since, as noted by Callinicos (2006: 69-70):

"Exploitation is a relational concept. Now mobility and immobility are best defined as relative one another, but this doesn't generate the right kind of relationship, since being mobile doesn't make one dependent on the immobile in the way in which, in Marx's theory of exploitation, the capitalist is dependent on the worker's labour".

The "right kind of relationship" is not produced by raw spatial mobility but rather by the ability to make social links successfully, and appropriate surplus that changes the balance of Relations of Production. To this extent, the notions of Means and Relations of Interaction fulfil the important role of bridging a Marxist concept of exploitation in a networked logic, preserving the centrality of social conflict in the explanation of change.

Although the framework so far proposed might seem abstract, it is actually aimed at discussing real-world interaction between different people and groups. Crucially these occurred not in the abstract void of the topological space, but in the real physical world. As already highlighted elsewhere in this volume (see Dawson and Iacono's Introduction and De Nardi infra), however, the notion of space that we need to embrace is not an aseptically Euclidean one, but rather one that acknowledges the contribution of a variety of social aspects to the definition of what is remote and close. Mere distance and transportation technology available blend with other ideas about vicinity and distance rooted in everyday practice, transforming the way 'place' and territory are seen by people. Certainly, we have noticed that in some cases, the ability (both technological and social) to cross distances and get from one point to another is something that improves one's (or a group's) position in Relations of Interaction. This is because travelling as a performance immediately conveys the power of actors. At a very basic evolutionary level 'moving' means being able bodied. Besides, anthropological enquiry has long acknowledged how very often horizontal, real world distance is often translated in vertical (read hierarchical) distance, frequently linking people that travel to a higher cosmological level (Helms 1993). Besides the performative aspects, it is also to be reminded that, more pragmatically, travelling also allows one to reach different places that are in turn connected with other places furthering the reach of their connections and more broadly new relations. From a political perspective, all these new relationships with their increased range potentially substantially modify power equilibriums and oust the very order that sustains within and between societies, creating the premises for social change.

Exempla

One of the reasons the difference in being hegemonic in the local (*i.e.* in Relations of Production) and in the supra-local (*i.e.* in Relations of Interaction) domain has not been noted so far resides in the fact that very often the same people and social groups were predominant in both fields. Archaeology, anthropology and other social and historical disciplines dealing with pre-modern societies have therefore tended to conflate this distinction in an omni-comprehensive category of elite, which included both dimensions. However, if we do try to operate the distinction here suggested (between Relations of Production and Relations of Interaction), it is indeed possible to recognise the developments outlined at work. These become more apparent since the later phases of prehistory and the beginning of ancient history, when disparities in technology and resources available to be invested in Means of Interaction become more visible.

In a sense, the evident diffusion of many cultural traits that archaeology has always had the ability to reveal can often be explained through the theory here discussed. For instance, during the second half of the second millennium BC, the so-called Mycenaean civilisation, characterised by a Tributary Mode of Production, started to entertain durable relationships with smaller kin-ordered communities to the west, in the Central Mediterranean. The larger amount of surplus available to the rulers of Mycenaean polities allowed them to spend considerable resources in a complex set of factors which included both the material means through which interaction occurred (sailing ships, a technology that was arguably unknown at this time in this portion of the Mediterranean, see Iacono 2019) as well as other aspects which can be more adequately categorised as 'presentation' expenses (some example might have included, for instance, dress, tools and garments worn by sea-captains leading negotiations; or the gifts that were to be offered to local chiefs and other intermediaries) and that all contribute to the notion previously described of hegemony in Relations of Interaction. This hegemony resulted in the appropriation over a vast area of some cultural traits, embodied in the import and local imitation of fine wheel-made pottery. Interestingly, these 'traits' broadly intended, were almost exclusively located in settlements on the coast that were therefore more directly exposed to the physical presence of Mycenaean ships and intermediaries. Likewise, when small Central Mediterranean communities increased the capital available to them (mostly obtained through exchanges with the Alpine area and the Northern Adriatic), it is possible to notice a partial inversion of cultural influence with goods, models and stylistic features moving from west to east (Iacono 2019: 140 – 146). Toward the end of the Bronze Age, the important role of areas potentially in contact both with the Northern Adriatic and with other zones of the Mediterranean to the west, led to the development of important nodes within this Central Mediterranean trade, which managed to acquire larger amounts of capital. The allocation of these resources in the hands of groups within societies active in trade arguably produced in some of these nodal centres important social modifications. These have some archaeological manifestation in the development of large buildings and a certain concentration of surplus in the form of metal (*i.e.* bronze) and the products of specialised agriculture (olive oil contained in large storage jars; see Iacono 2019: 198 – 210; Dawson infra).

Moving to history, the majority of the large processes of cultural appropriation in the Ancient world, or *-isations* (e.g. Hellenisation, Romanisation in the Mediterranean or Indianisation and Sinicisation of Asia) can potentially be explained through the elements of the theory outlined so far (Helms 1988: 140 – 143; Prag and Quinn 2013; Roth 2007). This of course does not eliminate the complex nature of cultural encounters entailed by them and that have been highlighted by many (for a summary of the discussion see Van Dommelen 2016; Mihailovic 2019) but actually the theory suggests a way to understand the general framework under which these occurred (Iacono 2019). In these historical examples, the complexity and the nested nature of cultural influences involved, makes it often very difficult to disentangle who influenced who, at what time and through what means.

As a consequence, discerning Means of Interaction and Modes of Interaction can become a very hard task. Situations of pristine cultural contact (or semi-pristine, after long periods of isolation) are more promising and possess the undoubted advantage of highlighting the mechanic of interaction in a less ambiguous way. The most obvious historical context that can be claimed as an example is the period of contact between Eurasian and American societies in the second half of the 2nd millennium AD (Ekholm-Friedman and Friedman 2008; Paterson 2011; Wolf 2010).

Within this large context, the fur trade undertaken by Europeans with North American people can potentially constitute an interesting example. As is well known, the fur trade with North America started in the 17th century AD Newfoundland, following an interest of European fisherman for those areas, and rapidly evolved becoming one of the main activities for indigenous people in the wider region (Wolf 2010: 158 – 163). Thinking about these early encounters, it is undoubted that the confrontation between the considerably larger tonnage of transatlantic European ships, even the small ones devoted to fishing, played a role, impressing hunters from the small communities of the Northwest. To this advantage, it is necessary to add that associated with the use from the part of Europeans of firearms. It cannot be doubted that in early encounters even assisting to the occasional use of guns might have produced a sense of reverential intimidation, which accrued the aura of power accompanying the foreigners. Both these factors (*i.e.* ships and guns) in terms of the approach here exposed produce an advantage in Relations of Interaction, and the fact that Europeans possessed both, clearly indicates they were hegemonic in their relations with the people they encountered. Such very basic psychological advantage was transformed in a social and economic one by the mechanism explored previously. Indeed, this advantage produced an increase in popularity of European goods, which become very sought after (Wolf 2010: 193). Becoming more popular, such goods increased the value of surplus of communities more exposed to European trade (and that therefore had more European goods, which, from the 18th century AD onward included guns) making them more prosperous, at least in the short term. In particular groups directly dealing with European traders, such as hunters and warriors, increased their capital potential (in the sense described *supra*). This, in turn, produced considerable modifications within the Relations of Production of local societies. Such a development can be glanced for instance in the case of Iroquois, originally a matrilineal and patrilineal, agrarian society who, through the main period of the fur trade, gradually transformed itself in a male-centred hunting group (Ensor 2013: 56; Wolf 2010: 167). In the most conspicuous cases European influence manifested itself in phenomena such as Kwakiutl potlatches, where vast amounts of riches were destroyed in the attempt to establish which chief had to be primary one and therefore controlled business with Europeans (Codere 1956; Ruyle 1973; Wolf 2010: 191). Finally, throughout the whole fur trade period, the activity of indigenous communities and Europeans alike, exhibited that networked logic previously described. This is the case for instance again of the Abenakis and Micsmacs who fought for assuming the role of trade middlemen (Calloway 1994: 40) or of the Iroquois, who tried for the same reasons to cut out populations such as the Hurons and who, in turn, where replaced later on by the Ottawa (Wolf 2010: 163, 169).

Another useful example, dating to approximately the same period is the encounter between the polity occupying the area to the south of the Congo River estuary (Kingdom of Kongo) and western colonial powers. Despite some sort of European contact had already occurred in the 14th century (resulting in the selective adoption of christinaity from the part of elites), conditions of relatively pristine interaction broadly similar to those described for the previous example are also met in this case (De Maret 2005; Thornton 2001). While the currency of fur trade was fur (or better fur wool) in the African case it was actually human beings, *i.e.* slaves (*e.g.* as attested by the use in Gabon of the term *peça* for slaves originally indicating a unit of cloth used as currency; see Bucher 1986: 143). In the area, the Kingdom of Kongo was a complex system of (predominantly) matrilineal societies that allowed social mobility through a combination of exchange of prestige goods for women and slaves (Ekholm-Friedman 2008; Thornton 2001). Relationships between local groups from this area, that is Relations of Interaction according to our terminology, were not balanced and the possibility for asymmetry was embedded in the very functioning of the system and essentially connected to greater availability of prestige goods. As Ekholm-Friedman puts it "Those groups which control the sources, production and distribution of prestige goods have dominant position" we might perhaps add here in Relations of Interaction, and again "the flow of these goods away from the sources of control is by far the most important mechanism of intergroup ranking" (Ekholm-Friedman 2008: 237). It is broadly acknowledged that the increase of contact with European colonial powers resulted in considerable transformations (Heywood 2009). The same psychological advantage in Relations of Interaction in favour of Europeans previously highlighted for the North American fur trade, applies also here (*e.g.* so high was the perception of Europeans that for instance the Lugbara of the Congo considered them as supernatural beings able to move at incredible speed; see Helms 1988: 62 – 3) increasing the perceived value of goods coming from the colonial powers. The competition for highly valued European goods, which were acquired in exchange for slaves, lead to the start of slave hunting on an unprecedented scale. This in turn produced the permanence of male offspring in chief residence and the acquisition of female slaves who made *de facto* a shift to patrilineality feasible. Also, since the King, who originally acted as a networker (in the sense previously explained), no longer had the power to control exchange in prestige goods, now flowing into communities through direct economic transactions with the Europeans, the very basis of hierarchy ceased to exist, thus favouring social mobility (similar conditions were also in Gabon, see Bucher 1986: 140). As a result the unity of the Kingdom of Kongo did not resist for long and at the end of the 18th century AD had almost completely lost any political importance (Ekholm-Friedman 2008: 248).

Conclusions

In this paper I have tried to highlight some of the limitations embedded in the so-called network standpoint as it has been developed in certain branches of social theory. I have argued that such a perspective, particularly when it flattens complex social phenomena in a bi-dimensional opposition between inclusion and exclusion, is not particularly effective. I have also argued that combining some aspects of the network approach with existing strands of social theory, in particular Marxist social theory, might offer a more effective alternative.

The kind of approach advanced, however, is far from representing Marxist orthodoxy and actually tries to incorporate many revisions derived from the western tradition of Marxism. A more inclusive notion of Means of Production has been adopted and on this basis I have proposed to analytically extend the same concept adopted by Marx for the analysis of the individual entity to the inter-societal domain. Through the concepts of Means, Relations and Modes of Interaction I have tried to analyse the possible social implications of interaction at the level of the individual society. Also through the adoption of some principles based on Social Network Analysis and Network Exchange Theory I have tried to make sense of the changes created by interactions between more than two actors in an interconnected whole.

I trust there is much potential for exploring the concepts of Means, Relations and Modes of Interaction in different historical contingencies, trying to see how, what we might call "the social logic of interaction", unfolds.

Bibliography

Ahmad, Y. 2006. The Scope and Definitions of Heritage: From Tangible to Intangible. *International Journal of Heritage Studies* 12(3): 292-300.

Albert, R. and Barabási, A.L. 2002. Statistical Mechanics of Complex Networks. *Review of Modern Physics* 74(47): 47-97.

Alberti, G. 2008. There is something Cypriot in the air. Some thoughts on the problem of the Base Ring pottery and other Cyprus-related items from (local) Middle Bronze Age contexts in Sicily. In A. McCarthy (ed.) *Island dialogues: Proceedings of the postgraduate Cypriot archaeology conference (POCA), 2006,* 130-153. University of Edinburgh: Edinburgh.

Alberti, L. and Bettelli, M. 2005. Contextual problems of Mycenaean pottery in Italy. In R. Laffineur and E. Greco (eds) *Emporia: Aegeans in the Central and Eastern Mediterranean, Proceedings of the 10th International Aegean Conference, Athens, Italian School of Archaeology, 14 – 18 April 2004,* 547-60. Liège and Austin, TX: Université de Liège, Histoire de l'Art et Archéologie de la Grèce Antique.

Alessandri, L. 2007. *L'occupazione costiera protostorica del Lazio centromeridionale.* Oxford: British Archaeological Reports.

Alessandri, L. 2013. *Latium Vetus in the Bronze Age and Early Iron Age / Il Latium Vetus nell'età del Bronzo e nella prima età del Ferro.* Oxford: British Archaeological Reports.

Alessandri, L. 2016. Hierarchical and federative polities in protohistoric Latium Vetus. An analysis of early states, territories and settlements in protohistoric central Italy. In P. Attema (ed.) *Proceedings of a specialist conference at the Groningen Institute of Archaeology of the University of Groningen,* 67-82. Groningen.

Al-Sayed, K., Turner, A., Hillier, B., Lida, S. and Penn, A. 2014. *Space Syntax Methodology: A Teaching Textbook for the MSc Spatial Design: Architecture & Cities.* London: UCL Discovery/Bartlett School of Architecture.

Althusser, L. 1969. *For Marx.* New York: Pantheon Books.

Amati, V., Shafie, T. and Brandes, U. 2017. Reconstructing Archaeological Networks with Structural Holes. *Journal of Archaeological Method and Theory* 25: 226-253.

Ambrose, W.R. 1976. Obsidian and its prehistoric distribution in Melanesia. In N. Barnard (ed.) *The Proceedings of a Symposium on Scientific Methods of Research in the the Study of Ancient Chinese Bronzes and Southeast Asian Metal and other Archaeological Artifacts,* 351-378. Melbourne: National Gallery of Victoria.

Ambrose, W.R. 1978. The Loneliness of the Long Distance Trader in Melanesia. *Mankind* 11: 326-333.

Anderson, A., Chappell, J., Gagan, M. and Grove, R. 2006. Prehistoric maritime migration in the Pacific islands: an hypothesis of ENSO forcing. *The Holocene* 16(1): 1-6.

Anderson, B. 2006. *Imagined Communities. The Origins and Spread of Nationalism.* London: Verso.

Anderson, C. 2008. The End of Theory: The Data Deluge Makes the Scientific Method Obsolete. https://www.wired.com/2008/06/pb-theory/

Anderson, K.B. 2010. *Marx at the Margins: On Nationalism, Ethnicity, and Non-Western Societies.* University of Chicago Press.

Anderson, P. 1976. The antinomies of Antonio Gramsci. *New Left Review* I, 100: 5-78.

Ardesia, V., Cattani, M., Marazzi, M. Nicoletti, F., Secondo, M. and Tusa, S. 2006. Gli scavi nell'abitato dell'età del Bronzo di Mursia, Pantelleria (TP). Relazione preliminare delle campagne 2001 – 2005. *Rivista di Scienze Preistoriche* 56: 1-75.

Arrighi, G. 1994. *The Long Twentieth Century: Money, Power, and the Origins of our Times.* London; New York: Verso.

Atzbach, R. 2016. Neue Zugänge zu alten Räumen auf dänischen Burgen: Relative Asymmetry. *Château Gaillard* 27: 21-26.

Autenrieth, S.N. 2015. Architektur und sozialer Raum. Space-Syntax-Analysen an Wirtshäusern. In D. Wehner and A. Wesse (eds) *Rasthäuser – Gasthäuser – Geschäftshäuser*. Universitätsforschungen zur prähistorischen Archäologie, 35-38. Bonn: Habelt.

Ayán Vila, X.M., Blanco Rotea, R. and Mañana Borrazás, P. (eds) 2003. *Archaeotecture: Archaeology of Architecture.* Oxford: Archaeopress.

Bachhuber, C. 2006. Aegean interest on the Uluburun ship. *American Journal of Archaeology* 110(3): 345-363.

Barabási, A.L. 2002. *Linked: The New Science of Networks.* Cambridge, Mass: Perseus Pub.

Barabási, A.L. 2010. *Bursts: The Hidden Pattern Behind Everything We Do.* New York, N.Y: Dutton Adult.

Barbieri, C., Sandoval, J.R., Valqui, J., Shimelman, A., Ziemendorff, S., Schröder, R., Geppert, M., Roewer, L., Gray, R., Stoneking, M., Fujita, R. and Heggarty, P. 2017. Enclaves of genetic diversity resisted Inca impacts on population history. *Scientific Reports* 7(1): 17411.

Barker, G. and Rasmussen, T. 1998. *The Etruscans.* Oxford: Blackwell.

Barth, F. 1969. Introduction. In F. Barth (ed.) *Ethnic Groups and Boundaries: The Social Organization of Culture Difference*, 9-30. Long Grove: Waveland Press.

Barthélemy, M. 2011. Spatial Networks. *Physics Reports* 499(1-3): 1-101.

Barthélemy, M. and Louf, R. 2017. *Morphogenesis of Spatial Networks.* Cham: Springer International Publishing / Springer International Publishing AG.

Bassett Smith, D. and Bullmore, E. 2006. Small-world Brain Networks. *The Neuroscientist* 12(6): 512-523.

Batty, M. 2013. *The New Science of Cities.* Cambridge, Mass.: MIT Press.

Baudrillard, J. 1975. *The Mirror of Production.* St. Louis: Telos Press.

Behan, T. 2009. *The Italian Resistance. Fascists, Guerrillas and the Allies.* London: Pluto Press.

Belardelli, C. 2007. *Repertorio dei siti Protostorici del Lazio. Province di Roma, Viterbo e Frosinone.* Florence: All'Insegna del Giglio.

Bentley, A.R., O'Brien, M.J. and Brock, A.B. 2014. Mapping collective behavior in the big-data era. *Behavioral and Brain Sciences* 37(01): 63-76.

Benton, T. 1989. Marxism and Natural Limits: An Ecological Critique and Reconstruction. *New Left Review* 1(178): 51-86.

Bernabò Brea L. 1957. *Sicily before the Greeks*. London: Thames and Hudson.

Bernabò Brea L. and Cavalier, M. 1968. *Meligunìs Lipára III*. Stazioni preistoriche delle isole Panarea, Salina e Stromboli. Palermo: Flaccovio.

Bernabò Brea L. and Cavalier, M. 1980. *Meligunìs Lipára IV. L'acropoli di Lipari nella preistoria.* Palermo: Flaccovio.

Bernabò Brea, L. and Cavalier, M. 1991. La tholos termale di San Calogero nell'isola di Lipari. *Studi Micenei ed Egeo-Anatolici* (1991): 1-78.

Bevan, A. and Wilson, A.G. 2013. Models of settlement hierarchy based on partial evidence. *Journal of Archaeological Science* 40: 2415-2427.

Bhabha, H.K. 1994. *The Location of Culture*. London; New York: Routledge.

Biagioli, C., De Chiara, M., Ferrari, E., Rana, A., Khan, S.A. and Vidale, M. 2016. A Guide to Kandak and Kotah Valleys. A Field Companion to "Talking Stones". *ACT Reports and Memoirs* 4. Lahore: Sang-e-Meel.

Bietti Sestieri, A.M. 1988. The 'Mycenaean connection' and its impact on the central Mediterranean societies. *Dialoghi di Archeologia* 6: 23-51.

Bietti Sestieri, A.M. 2008. L'Età del Bronzo Finale nella Penisola Italiana. *Padusa* 44: 7-54.

Bietti Sestieri, A.M. 2010. *L'Italia nell'Età del Bronzo e del Ferro. Dalle Palafitte a Romolo*. Rome: Carocci.

Bietti Sestieri, A.M. 2013. The Bronze Age in Sicily. In H. Fokkens and A. Harding (eds) *The Oxford Handbook of the European Bronze Age*, 653-667. Oxford: Oxford University Press.

Bietti Sestieri, A.M. 2015. Sicily in Mediterranean History in the Second Millennium BC. In A.B. Knapp and P. Van Dommelen (eds) *The Cambridge Prehistory of the Bronze and Iron Age Mediterranean*, 74-95. Cambridge: Cambridge University Press.

Blake, E. 2005. The Mycenaeans in Italy. A minimalist perspective. *Papers of the British School at Rome* 76: 1-34.

Blake, E. 2014. *Social Networks and Regional Identity in Bronze Age Italy*. New York, NY: Cambridge University Press.

Blake, E. and Knapp, B. (eds) 2004. *The Archaeology of Mediterranean Prehistory: The Archaeology of Mediterranean Prehistory*. Oxford: Blackwell Publishing.

Blanchard, P. and Volchenkov, D. 2009. *Mathematical Analysis of Urban Spatial Networks*. Berlin: Springer.

Boccaletti, S., Latora, V., Moreno, Y., Chavez, M. and Hwang, D.-U. 2006. Complex networks: structure and dynamics. *Physics Reports* 424: 175-308.

Boltanski, L. and Chiapello, E. 2005. *The New Spirit of Capitalism*. London; New York: Verso.

Bonanno, A. 2008. Insularity and isolation: Malta and Sicily in Prehistory. In A. Bonanno and P. Militello (eds) *Malta negli Iblei, gli Iblei a Malta*, 27-37. Palermo: Progetto KASA, Officina di Studi Medievali.

Bonghi Jovino, M. 2005. Città e territorio: Veio, Tarquinia, Cerveteri e Vulci. Appunti e riconsiderazioni. In O. Paoletti and G. Camporeale (eds) *Dinamiche di sviluppo delle città nell'Etruria Meridionale: Veio, Caere, Tarquinia, Vulci. Atti del XXIII Convegno* di Studi Etruschi ed Italici, Roma, Veio, Cerveteri/Pyrgi, Tarquinia, Tuscania, Vulci, Viterbo. 1 – 6 Ottobre 2001, 27-58. Pisa. Istituti Editoriali e Poligrafici Internazionali.

Bonghi Jovino, M. 2008. *Tarquinia etrusca. Tarconte e il primato della città.* Rome: L'Erma di Bretschneider.

Borgatti, S.P. and Everett, M.G. 2006. A Graph-theoretic perspective on centrality. *Social Networks* 28(4): 466-484.

Borgatti, S.P. and Halgin, D.S. 2011. On Network Theory. *Organization Science Articles in Advance* 22(5): 1168-1181.

Borgatti, S.P. and Lopez-Kidwell, V. 2014. Network Theory. In J. Scott and P. J. Carrington (eds) *The Sage Handbook of Social Network Analysis*, 40-51. London: SAGE Publications.

Börner, W. and Uhlirz, S. (eds) 2014. *Proceedings of the 18th International Conference on Cultural Heritage and New Technologies 2013.* Wien.

Bourdieu, P. 1986. The forms of Capital. In J. G. Richardson (ed.) *Handbook of Theory and Research for the Sociology of Education*, 241-58. New York: Greenwood.

Braudel, P. 1972. *The Mediterranean and the Mediterranean World in the Age of Philip II.* London: Collins.

Branigan, K. 1981. Minoan Colonialism. *The Annual of the British School at Athens* 76: 23-35.

Branigan, K. 1984. Minoan Community Colonies in the Aegean? In R. Hägg and N. Marinatos (eds) *The Minoan Thalassocracy: Myth and Reality*, 49-53. Paul Aström Vörlag.

Branigan, K.M. 1990. An Early Aegean Gateway Community. In R. Laffineur and L. Basch (eds) *Thalassa. L'Égée Préhistorique et la Mer, Actes de la 3e Rencontre Égéenne Internationale de l'Université de Liège*, 97-105. Liège and Austin: Université de Liège, Histoire de l'Art et Archéologie de la Grèce Antique.

Brocato, P. 2000. *La necropoli etrusca della Riserva del Ferrone.* Rome: Quasar.

Broodbank, C. 2000. *An island archaeology of the early Cyclades.* Cambridge: Cambridge University Press.

Broodbank, C. 2004. Minoanisation. *Proceedings of the Cambridge Philological Society* 50: 46-91.

Broodbank, C. 2006. The Origins and Early Development of Mediterranean Maritime Activity. *Journal of Mediterranean Archaeology* 19(2):199-230.

Broodbank, C. 2013. *The Making of the Middle Sea. A History of the Mediterranean from the Beginning to the Emergence of the Classical World.* London: Thames and Hudson.

Brughmans, T. 2010. Connecting the Dots: Towards an Archaeological Network Analysis. *Oxford Journal of Archaeology* 29(3): 277-303.

Brughmans, T. 2012. Thinking through Networks: A Review of Formal Network Methods in Archaeology. *Journal of Archaeological Method and Theory* 20(4): 623-62.

Brusasco, P. 2004. Theory and Practice in the Study of Mesopotamian Domestic Space. *Antiquity* 78(299): 142-157.

Bucher, H. 1986. *The Atlantic Slave Trade and the Gabon Estuary: The Mpongwe to 1860.* In P. D. Curtin and P. E. Lovejoy (eds) *Africans in Bondage: Studies in Slavery and the Slave Trade. Essays in Honor of Philip D. Curtin on the Occasion of the Twenty-fifth Anniversary of African Studies at the University of Wisconsin*, 25-8. Madison, Wis: African Studies Program, University of Wisconsin.

Callinicos, A. 2006. *The Resources of Critique*. Cambridge; Malden, MA: Polity.

Calloway, C.G. 1990. *The Western Abenakis of Vermont, 1600-1800: War, Migration, and the Survival of an Indian People*. Norman: University of Oklahoma Press.

Cappelletto, F. 2005. Personal memories and personal stories. Recalling the Nazi-Fascist massacres. In F. Cappelletto (ed.) *Memory and World War Two. An Ethnographic Approach*, 101-30. Oxford: Berg.

Carafa, P. 2014. I Latini. Prospettiva Archeologica. In M. Aberson, M.C. Biella, M. Di Fazio and M. Wullschleger (eds) *Entre Archéologie et Histoire: Dialogues sur divers peuples de L'Italie Préromaine*, 31-50. Berlin: Peter Lang.

Carandini, A. 1997. *La nascita di Roma. Dei, Lari, eroi e uomini all'alba di una civiltà*. Torino: Giulio Einaudi.

Carrier, J.G. and Kalb, D. (eds) 2015. *Anthropologies of Class: Power, Practice and Inequality*. Cambridge, United Kingdom: Cambridge University Press.

Cassitti, P. 2016. Aspekte globaler Zirkulation von Kupfer und Messing Aspekte globaler Zirkulation von Kupfer und Messing in der frühen Neuzeit: Ein Beitrag zur Erforschung transeuropäischer Handelsrouten. *Mitteilungen der Deutschen Gesellschaft für Archäologie des Mittelalters und der Neuzeit* (29): 285-294.

Castells, M. 1996. *The Rise of the Network Society*. Malden, Mass: Blackwell Publishers.

Cattani, M., Nicoletti, F. and Tusa, S. 2012. Resoconto preliminare degli scavi dell'insediamento di Mursia (Pantelleria). In *Atti della XLI Riunione scientifica "Dai ciclopi agli ecisti: società e territorio nella Sicilia preistorica e protostorica", San Cipirello (PA), 16 – 19 novembre 2006*, 637-651. Firenze: Istituto Italiano di Preistoria e Protostoria.

Cazzella, A., Levi, S. and Williams, J.L. 1997. The petrographic examination of impasto pottery from Vivara and the Aeolian Islands: a case of inter-island pottery exchange in the Bronze Age of southern Italy. *Origini. Preistoria e protostoria delle civiltà antiche* 21: 187-205.

Cazzella, A. and Recchia, G. 2009. The 'Mycenaeans' in the central Mediterranean: a comparison between the Adriatic and the Tyrrhenian seaways. *Pasiphae* 3: 27-40.

Cazzella, A. and Recchia, G. 2012. Eolie, Malta e le reti di scambio tra gli ultimi secoli del III e gli inizi del I millennio a.C. In *Atti della XLI Riunione scientifica "Dai ciclopi agli ecisti: società e territorio nella Sicilia preistorica e protostorica", San Cipirello (PA), 16 – 19 novembre 2006*, 1001-1013. Firenze: Istituto Italiano di Preistoria e Protostoria.

Chapman, R. 2014. Scales, interaction and movement in later Mediterranean prehistory. In S. Souvatzi (ed.) *Space and Time in Mediterranean Prehistory and Beyond*, 32-48. New York, Abingdon: Routledge.

Chase-Dunn, C. and Hall, T.D. 1997. *Rise and Demise: Comparing World Systems*. Boulder, Colorado: Westview Press.

Chatford Clark, D.L. 2007. Viewing the liturgy: a space syntax study of changing visibility and accessibility in the development of the Byzantine church in Jordan. *World Archaeology* 39(1): 84-104.

Chevallier, R. 1976. *Roman Roads*. London: BT Batsford Limited.

Clark, G. 2000. Mid-sequence isolation in Fiji 2500 – 1000 BP. *IPPA Bulletin* 19: 152-158.

Classen, C. and Howes, D. 2007. The Sensescape of the Museum: Western Sensibilities and Indigenous Artifacts. In E. Edwards, C. Gosden, and R. Phillips (eds) *Sensible Objects: Colonialism, Museums and Material Culture*, 199-220. Oxford: Berg

Claval, P. 1984. The Concept of Social Space and the Nature of Social Geography. *New Zealand Geographer* 40(2): 105-9.

Claval, P. 1993. Marxism and Space. *L'Espace Géographique* 1(1): 73-96.

Cline, E.H. 1995. "'My Brother, My Son': Rulership and Trade between the LBA Aegean, Egypt and the Near East". In P. Rehak (ed.) *The Role of the Ruler in the Prehistoric Aegean, Proceedings of a Panel Discussion Presented at the Annual Meeting of the Archaeological Institute of America, New Orleans, Luisiana, 28 December 1992. Aegaeum 11*, 143-150. Liège and Austin, TX: Université de Liège, Histoire de l'Art et Archéologie de la Grèce Antique.

Cline, E.H. 2005. The multivalent nature of imported objects in the ancient Mediterranean world. In R. Laffineur and E. Greco (eds) *Emporia: Aegeans in the central and eastern Mediterranean, proceedings of the 10th international Aegean conference, Athens, Italian School of Archaeology, 14 – 18 April 2004*, 45-51. Liège and Austin, TX: Université de Liège, Histoire de l'Art et Archéologie de la Grèce Antique.

Cline, E.H. 2013. Aegean-Near East relations in the second millennium BC. In J. Aruz, S. B. Graff, and Rakic (eds) *Cultures in Contact: From Mesopotamia to the Mediterranean in the Second Millennium BC*, 26-33. NY: The Metropolitan Museum of Art New York.

Codere, H. 1956. The amiable side of Kwakiutl life: The potlatch and the play potlatch. *American Anthropologist* 58(2): 334-351.

Cohen, G.A. 2000. *Karl Marx's Theory of History: A Defence Expanded*. Princeton, NJ: Princeton University Press.

Collar, A., Coward, F., Brughmans, T. and Mills, B.J. 2015. Networks in Archaeology: Phenomena, Abstraction, Representation. *Journal of Archaeological Method and Theory* 22(1): 1-32.

Colonna, G. (ed.) 1976. *Civiltà del Lazio Primitivo (exhibition catalogue)*. Roma: Multigrafica Editrice.

Copat, V., Danesi, M. and Recchia, G. 2010. Isolation and interaction cycles. Small Mediterranean islands from the Neolithic to the Bronze age. *Shima – The International Journal of Research into Island Cultures* 4(2): 41-64.

Cornell, P. and Fahlander, F. (eds) 2007. *Encounters, Materialities, Confrontations: Archaeologies of Social Space and Interaction*. Newcastle, UK: Cambridge Scholars Press.

Cospito, G. 2004. Egemonia. In F. Frosini and G. Liguori (eds) *Le parole di Gramsci: per un lessico dei Quaderni del carcere*, 74-92. Roma: Carocci.

Cox, R.W. 1983. Gramsci, Hegemony and International Relations: An Essay in Method. *Millennium – Journal of International Studies* 12(2): 162-175.

Craane, M.L. 2013. *Spatial Patterns; The Late-Medieval and Early-Modern Economy of the Bailiwick of 's Hertogenbosch from an Interregional, Regional and Local Spatial Perspective*. Unpublished PhD Thesis, Tilburg University.

Crehan, K. 2002. *Gramsci, Culture and Anthropology*. Berkeley and Los Angeles: University of California Press.

Crouch, D. 2015. Affect, Heritage, Feeling. In E. Waterton and S. Watson (eds) *The Palgrave Handbook of Contemporary Heritage Research*, 177-90. Palgrave Macmillan.

Crumley, C. and Marquadt, W. 1987. *Regional Dynamics: Burgundia Landscapes in Historical Perspectives*. San Diego: Academic Press.

Cunliffe, B. 2017. *On the Ocean. The Mediterranean and the Atlantic from Prehistory to AD 1500*. Oxford: Oxford University Press.

Cutting, M. 2003. The Use of Spatial Analysis to Study Prehistoric Settlement Architecture. *Oxford Journal of Archaeology* 22(1): 1-21.

Dafinger, A. 2004. *Anthropologie des Raumes: Untersuchungen zur Beziehung räumlicher und sozialer Ordnung im Süden Burkina Fasos.* Köln: Rüdiger Köppe.

D'Agata, A.L. 2000. Interactions between Aegean groups and local communities in Sicily in the Bronze Age: the evidence from pottery. *Studi Micenei ed Egeo-Anatolici* 42: 61-83.

Dawson, H. 2016. Brave New Worlds: Islands, place-making, and connectivity in the Bronze Age Mediterranean. In B. Molloy and R. Doonan (eds) *Of Odysseys and Oddities. Scales and modes of interaction between prehistoric Aegean societies and their neighbours*, 323-42. Sheffield

Dawson, H. 2019. As good as it gets? "Optimal" Marginality in the Longue Durée of the Mediterranean Islands. *Journal of Eastern Mediterranean and Heritage Studies* 7(4): 451-465.

Dawson, H. 2020. Network science and island archaeology: Advancing the debate. *The Journal of Island and Coastal Archaeology*. DOI: 10.1080/15564894.2019.1705439.

Dawson, H. and Nikolakopoulou, I. 2020. East meets West: Exchange and identities in the Bronze Age Mediterranean. *E-Topoi Special Volume* 7: 155-192.

Dawson, P.C. 2000. Space Syntax Analysis of Central Inuit Snow Houses. *Journal of Anthropological Archaeology* 21(4): 464-480.

De Angelis, F. (ed.) 2013. *Regionalism and Globalism in Antiquity*. Colloquia Antiqua 7. Leuven: Peeters.

De Certeau, M. 1984. *The Practice of Everyday Life*. London: Penguin.

De La Haye, Y., Marx, K. and Engels, F. 1980. *Marx and Engels on the means of communication: (the movement of commodities, people, information and capital): a selection of texts*. New York: International General.

De Landa, M. 2006. *A New Philosophy of Society: Assemblage Theory and Social Complexity*. London; New York: Continuum.

De Maret, P. 2005. From pottery groups to ethnic groups in Central Africa. In A. B. Stahl (ed) *African Archaeology: A Critical Introduction*. Studies in Global Archaeology, 420-40. Malden, MA: Blackwell.

Deleuze, G. and Guattari, F. 2004. *A Thousand Plateaus: Capitalism and Schizophrenia*. London: Continuum.

Della Fina, G.M. and Pellegrini, E. 2013. *Da Orvieto a Bolsena. Un percorso tra Etruschi e Romani*. Pisa: Pacini Editore.

De Nardi, S. 2016. *The Poetics of Conflict Experience. Materiality and Embodiment in Second World War Italy*. London: Routledge.

De Nardi, S. 2017. Emplacing the Italian resistance. In N. Saunders and P. Cornish (eds) *Modern Conflict and the Senses*, 152-144. London, Routledge.

de Pina-Cabral, J. 1989. The Mediterranean as a category of regional comparison: A critical approach. *Current Anthropology* 30(3): 399-406.

Dhoop, T. 2014. Man, Ships, Harbours and Towns. Exploring the Impact of Maritime Commerce on Urban Topography in 12th to 14th Century Europe. In B. Gibson, M. Jonk, and J. Found (eds) *Sea Lines of Communication Conference Proceedings*, 109-127. Southampton: University of Southampton.

Diamond, J. 2000. Taiwan's gift to the world. *Nature* 403: 709-710.

Diani, M. and McAdam, D. 2003. *Social Movements and Networks: Relational Approaches to Collective Action*. Oxford: Oxford University Press.

Domanska, E. 2005. The material presence of the past. *History and Theory* 45(3): 337-348.

Donnelan, L. (ed.) 2020. *Archaeological Networks and Social Interaction*. London-New York: Routledge.

Donohue, M. and Denham, T. 2010. Farming and language in Island Southeast Asia. *Current Anthropology* 51(2): 223-256.

Döring, J. and Thielmann, T. 2009. *Spatial Turn: Das Raumparadigma in den Kultur- und Sozialwissenschaften* 2., unveränd. Aufl. Bielefeld: Transcript.

van Dyke, R.M. 1999. Space Syntax Analysis at the Chacoan Outlier of Guadalupe. *American Antiquity* 64(3): 461-473.

Earle, T. 2011. Paths and roads in evolutionary perspective. In C.D. Trombold (ed.) *Ancient Road Networks and Settlement Hierarchies in the New World*, 10-17. New York-Cambridge: Cambridge University Press.

Eder, B. and Jung, R. 2005. On the character of social relationships between Greece and Italy in the 12th/11th century BC. In R. Laffineur and E. Greco (eds) *Emporia: Aegeans in the Central and Eastern Mediterranean. Proceedings of the 10th International Aegean Conference*, 485-495. Athens: Italian School of Archaeology.

Ekholm-Friedman, K. 2008. External Exchange and the Transformation of Central African Social Systems. In K. Ekholm-Friedman and J. Friedman (eds) *Historical Transformations: The Anthropology of Global Systems*, 231-54. Lanham: AltaMira Press.

Ekholm-Friedman, K. and Friedman, J. (eds) 2008. *Historical Transformations: The Anthropology of Global Systems*. Lanham: AltaMira Press.

Emirbayer, M. 1997. Manifesto for a relational sociology. *American Journal of Sociology* 103(2): 281-317.

Enei, F. 2001. *Progetto Ager Caeretanus. Il litorale di Alsium: ricognizioni archeologiche nel territorio di Ladispoli, Cerveteri e Fiumicino (Alsium-Caere-Ad Turres-Ceri)*. Roma: Comune di Ladispoli.

Ensor, B. 2013. *The Archaeology of Kinship: Advancing Interpretation and Contributions to Theory*. Tucson: The University of Arizona Press.

Etzlaub, E. 1990. *Das sein dy landstrassen durch das Romisch reych von einem Kunigreych zw dem andern dy an Tewtsche land stossen von meilen zw meiln mit puncten verzaichnet*. Berlin: Deutscher Verlag der Wissenschaften.

Evans, T. 2013. What makes a site important? Centrality, gateways, and gravity. In C. Knappett (ed.) *Network Analysis in Archaeology. New Approaches to Regional Interaction*, 125-150. Oxford: Oxford University Press.

Evans, T. and Rivers, R. 2017. Was Thebes necessary? Contingency in Spatial Modeling. *Frontiers of Digital Humanities* 4,8, DOI: 10.3389/fdigh.2017.00008.

Faier, L. and Rofel, L. 2014. Ethnographies of Encounter. *Annual Review of Anthropology* 43(1): 363-77.

Fairclough, G. 1992. Meaningful Constructions – Spatial and Functional Analysis of Medieval Buildings. *Antiquity* (66): 348-366.

Faupel, F. 2018. Reconstructing Early Iron Age pathways in the Upper Rhine valley. In J. Wilczek, A. Cannot, T. Le Cozanet, J. Remy, J. Macháček, J. Klápště (eds) *Interdisciplinarity and New Approaches in the Research of the Iron Age, Supplementum IV*, 109-113. Vydání Brno: Masarykova Univerzita.

Faupel, F. and Nakoinz, O. 2018. Rekonstruktion des Wegesystems und Identifikation von Wegparametern der Bronzezeit in Schleswig-Holstein. In B. Nessel, D. Neumann, and M. Bartelheim (eds) *Bronzezeitlicher Transport – Akteure, Mittel und Wege*, 149-268. Tübingen: Tübingen University Press.

Filet, C. 2017. An Attempt to Estimate the Impact of Economic Flows on Latenian urbanization. *Frontiers Digital Humanities*. https://doi.org/10.3389/fdigh.2016.00010.

Fisher, K.D. 2014. Investigating Monumental Social Space in Late Bronze Age Cyprus: An Integrative Approach. In E. Paliou, U. Lieberwirth, and S. Polla (eds) *Spatial Analysis and Social Spaces*, 167-202. Berlin: De Gruyter.

Foster, J.B. 2000. *Marx's Ecology: Materialism and Nature*. New York: Monthly Review Press.

Foster, S.M. 1989. Analysis of Spatial Patterns in Buildings (Access Analysis) as an Insight into Social Structure: Examples from the Scottish Atlantic Iron Age. *Antiquity* (63): 40-50.

Fragnoli, P. 2012. *Circolazione e produzione della ceramica nei contesti Capo Graziano (BA – BM2) delle Isole Eolie*. Unpublished PhD Thesis. Università degli Studi di Ferrara.

Fragnoli, P. and Levi, S. 2011. Petrographic analysis of pottery from Pyla-Kokkinokremos. Preliminary report. In V. Karageorghis and O. Kouka (eds) *On cooking pots, drinking cups, loomweights, and ethnicity in Bronze Age Cyprus and neighbouring regions. An international archaeological symposium held in Nicosia, November 7th 2010*, 101-106. Nicosia: The A.G. Leventis Foundation.

Frank, A.G. 1993. Bronze Age World System Cycles. *Current Anthropology* 34(4): 383-429.

Franz, G. and Wiener, J.M. 2005. Exploring Isovist-Based Correlates of Spatial Behavior and Experience. In A. van Nes (ed) *5th International Space Syntax Symposium Proceedings*, 503-517. West Lafayette and Ashland: Purdue University Press and Atlas Books Distribution.

Freeman, L.C. 1979. Centrality in social networks conceptual clarification. *Social networks* 1(3): 215-239.

Friedman, J. 1974. Marxism, structuralism and vulgar materialism. *Man* 9(3): 444-469.

Friedman, J. 2008. Marxist theory and systems of total reproduction. In K. Ekholm-Friedman and J. Friedman (eds) *Historical Transformations: The Anthropology of Global Systems*, 31-42. Lanham: AltaMira Press.

Fulminante, F. 2012. Social Network Analysis and the emergence of central Places: A case study from central Italy (Latium vetus). *BaBesch* 87:1-27.

Fulminante, F. 2014. *The Urbanization of Rome and Latium Vetus from the Bronze Age to the Archaic Era*. Cambridge: Cambridge University Press.

Fulminante, F. 2017. Coordinated and unbalanced powers. How Latin cities shaped their terrestrial transportation network. *Frontiers of Digital Humanities* https://doi.org/10.3389/fdigh.2017.00004.

Fulminante, F. 2018. The Latins. In G. D. Farney and G. Bradley (eds) *The peoples of Ancient Italy*, 473-497. Berlin; Boston: De Gruyter.

Fulminante, F. forthcoming. *Nucleated settlements as assemblages: A regional network approach to built environments. "What if we build this here?"*. In R. Salisbury and G. Attila (eds) *Spatial patterns, community organization and identity at nucleated settlements*. Suny Buffalo.

Fulminante, F. 2021. *The Rise of Early Rome: Transportation Networks and Domination in Central Italy, 1050-500 BC*. Cambridge: Cambridge University Press.

Fulminante, F. and Stoddart, S. 2012. Indigenous Political Dynamics and Identity from a Comparative Perspective: Etruria and Latium vetus. In E. Alberti and S. Sabatini (eds) *Exchange Networks and Local Transformations. Interactions and Local Changes in Europe and the Mediterranean from the Bronze Age to the Iron Age*, 117-133. Oxford: Oxbow Books.

Gaffney, D., Summerhayes, G.R., Ford, A., Scott, J.M., Denham, T., Field, J. and Dickinson, W. 2015. Earliest pottery on New Guinea mainland reveals Austronesian influences in highland environments 3000 years ago. *PLoS ONE* 10(9) https://doi.org/10.1371/journal.pone.0134497

Geys, B. and Murdoch, Z. 2010. Measuring the 'Bridging' versus 'Bonding' nature of Social Networks: A proposal for Integrating existing measures. *Sociology-the Journal of The British Sociological Association* 44(3): 523-540.

Gibson, B., Jonk, M. and Found, J. (eds) 2014. *Sea Lines of Communication Conference Proceedings*. Southampton: University of Southampton.

Giardino, C. 2000. Sicilian hoards and protohistoric metal trade in the central west Mediterranean. In C. F. E. Pare (ed.) *Metals make the world go round. The supply and circulation of metals in Bronze Age Europe*, 99-107. Oxford: Oxbow Books.

Gilchrist, R. 1994. *Gender and Material Culture: The Archaeology of Religious Women* 1. publ. London and New York: Routledge.

Girvan, M. and Newman, M.E.J. 2002. Community structure in social and biological networks. *Proceedings of the National Academy of Sciences of the United States of America* 99(12): 7821-7826.

Godelier, M. 1999. *The Enigma of the Gift*. Chicago: University of Chicago Press.

Goffman, E. 1956. *The Presentation of Self in Everyday Life*. Edinburgh: University of Edinburgh, Social Sciences Research Centre.

Golitko, M., Schauer, M. and Terrell, J.E. 2012. Identification of Fergusson Island Obsidian on the Sepik Coast of Northern Papua New Guinea. *Archaeology in Oceania* 47: 151-156.

Golitko, M., Schauer, M. and Terrell, J.E. 2013. Obsidian Acquisition on the Sepik Coast of Northern Papua New Guinea During the Last Two Millennia. In G. Summerhayes and H. Buckley (eds) *Pacific Archaeology: Documenting the Past 50,000 years*, 43-57. Dunedin: University of Otago.

Gosden, C. 1995. Arboriculture and Agriculture in Coastal Papua New Guinea. *Antiquity* 69: 807-817.

Graeber, D. 2001. *Toward an Anthropological Theory of Value: The False Coin of Our Own Dreams*. New York: Palgrave.

Graham, S. 2006. Networks, agent-based models and the Antonine Itineraries. Implications for Roman Archaeology. *Journal of Mediterranean Archaeology* 19: 45-64.

Graham, S. and Weingart, S. 2015. The Equifinality of Archaeological Networks: An Agent-Based Exploratory Lab Approach. *Journal of Archaeological Method and Theory* 22(1): 248-74.

Gramsci, A. 1971. *Selections from the Prison Notebooks of Antonio Gramsci*. London: Lawrence and Wishart.

Granovetter, M. 1973. The Strength of Weak Ties. *American Journal of Sociology* 78(6): 1360-1380.

Graziadio, G. and Guglielmino, R. 2011. The Aegean and Cypriot imports to Italy as evidence for direct and indirect trade in the 14th and 13th centuries BC. In K. Duistermaat and I. Regulski (eds) *Intercultural Contacts in the Ancient Mediterranean. Proceedings of the International Conference at the Netherlands-Flemish Institute in Cairo, 25th to 29th October*, 309-326. Leuven: Orientalia Lovaniensia Analecta.

Gregory, C.A. 1982. *Gifts and Commodities*. London: Academic Press.

Gregory, D.J. and Urry, J. 1985. *Social Relations and Spatial Structures*. Basingstoke; London: Macmillan.

Groenhuijzen, M.R. and Verhagen, P. 2016. Testing the Robustness of Local Network Metrics in Research on Archeological Local Transport Networks. *Frontiers of Digital Humanities* https://doi.org/10.3389/fdigh.2016.00006.

Guglielmino, R. 2003. Il sito di Roca Vecchia: testimonianze di contatti con l'Egeo. In F. Lenzi (ed.) *L'Archeologia dell'Adriatico dalla Preistoria al Medioevo. Atti del Convegno Internazionale, Ravenna, 7 – 9 Giugno 2001*, 91-119. Firenze: All'Insegna del Giglio.

Guglielmino, R. 2005. Rocavecchia: nuove testimonianze di relazioni con l'Egeo e il Mediterraneo orientale nell'età del Bronzo. In R. Laffineur and E. Greco (eds) *Emporia: Aegeans in the Central and Eastern Mediterranean, Proceedings of the 10th International Aegean Conference, Athens, Italian School of Archaeology, 14 – 18 April 2004*, 637-651. Liège and Austin, TX: Université de Liège, Histoire de l'Art et Archéologie de la Grèce Antique.

Guglielmino, R., Levi, S.T. and Jones, R. 2010. Relations between the Aegean and Apulia in the Late Bronze Age: the evidence from an archaeometric study of the pottery at Roca (Lecce). *Rivista di Scienze Preistoriche* 40: 257-282.

Guidi, A. 1982. Sulle prime fasi dell'urbanizzazione nel Lazio protostorico. *Opus. Rivista internazionale per la storia economica e sociale dell'Antichità* 1(2): 279-289.

Guidi, A. 1985. An application of the Rank-Size rule to proto-historic settlement in the middle Tyrrhenian area. In S. Stoddart and C. Malone (eds) *Pattern in proto-history. Papers in Italian Archaeology* 4(3): 217 – 242.

Guidi, A. forthcoming. Urbanizzazione in Etruria meridionale e Latium vetus durante la Prima età del Ferro: la prospettiva dei Networks. In B. Barbaro (ed.) *Volume in memoria di Renato Peroni*.

Hacıgüzeller, P. and Thaler, U. 2014. Three Tales of Two Cities? A Comparative Analysis of Topological, Visual and Metric Properties of Archaeological Space in Malia and Pylos. In E. Paliou, U. Lieberwirth, and S. Polla (eds) *Spatial Analysis and Social Spaces*, 203-262. Berlin: De Gruyter.

Halbwachs, M. 1992. *On Collective Memory*. Chicago: Chicago University Press.

Hall, T.D., Kardulias, P.N. and Chase-Dunn, C. 2011. World-Systems Analysis and Archaeology: Continuing the Dialogue. *Journal of Archaeological Research* 19: 233-279.

Hanson, J. and Hillier, B. 1987. The Architecture of Community: Some New Proposals on the Social Consequences of Architectural and Planning Decisions. *Architecture et Comportement/Architecture and Behavior* 3(3): 251-273.

Harding, A. 2013. World Systems, Cores, and Peripheries in Prehistoric Europe. *European Journal of Archaeology* 16(3): 378-400.

Harding, T.G. 1967. *Voyagers of the Vitiaz Strait: A Study of a New Guinea Trade System.* Seattle: University of Washington Press.

Harding T.G. 1994. Precolonial New Guinea trade. *Ethnology* 33(2): 101-125.

Harris, O. 2014. Re-assembling communities. *Journal of Archaeological Method and Theory* 21: 76-94.

Harvey, D. 1994. The social construction of space and time. *Geographical Review of Japan* 67(2): 126-35.

Harvey, D. 2001. Heritage pasts and heritage presents: Temporality, meaning and the scope of heritage studies. *International Journal of Heritage Studies* 7(4): 319-338.

Hebblewhite, W.H.J. 2012. 'Means of communication as means of production' revisited. tripleC: Communication, capitalism and critique. *Open Access Journal for a Global Sustainable Information Society* 10(2): 203-213.

Heggarty, P. 2007. Linguistics for Archaeologists: Principles, Methods and the Case of the Incas. *Cambridge Archaeological Journal* 17(3): 311-340.

Helms, M.W. 1988. *Ulysses' sail: An ethnographic odyssey of power, knowledge, and geographical distance.* Princeton, N.J.; Guildford: Princeton University Press.

Helms, M.W. 1993. *Craft and the Kingly Ideal: Art, Trade, and Power.* University of Texas Press.

Henare, A., Halbraad, M. and Wastell, S. 2007. Introduction. In A. Henare, M. Holbraad, and S. Wastell (eds) *Thinking Through Things: Theorising Artefacts Ethnographically*, 1-31. London: Routledge.

Herzog, I. 2013. Least-cost networks. In G. Earl, T. Sly, A. Chrysanthi, P. Murrieta-Flores, C. Papadopoulos, I. Romanowska and I. Wheatley (eds) *CAA 2012. Proceedings of the 40th Annual Conference of Computer Applications and Quantitative Methods in Archaeology Southampton, 26-30 March 2012*, 240-51. Amsterdam: Pallas Publications.

Heywood, L.M. 2009. Slavery and its Transformation in the Kingdom of Kongo: 1491-1800. *The Journal of African History* 50(1): 1-22.

Hillebrandt, F. 2014. *Soziologische Praxistheorien: Eine Einführung.* Wiesbaden: Springer VS.

Hillier, B. 1996a. Cities as Movement Economies. *Urban Design International* 1(1): 41-60.

Hillier, B. 1996b. *Space is the Machine: A Configurational Theory of Architecture.* Cambridge: Cambridge University Press.

Hillier, B. 2009. Spatial Sustainability in Cities: Organic Patterns and Sustainable Forms. In D. Koch, L. Marcus and J. Steen (eds) *Proceedings of the 7th International Space Syntax Symposium.* TRITA-ARK-Forskningspublikation, 1-20. Stockholm: KTH.

Hillier, B. 2014. Spatial Analysis and Cultural Information: The need for theory as well as method in Space Syntax Analysis. In E. Paliou, U. Lieberwirth and S. Polla (eds) *Spatial Analysis and Social Spaces*, 19-48. Berlin: De Gruyter.

Hillier, B. and Hanson, J. 1984. *The Social Logic of Space.* Cambridge: Cambridge University Press.

Hirth, K.G. 1978. Interregional trade and the formation of prehistoric gateway communities. *American Antiquity* 43: 35-45.

Hodos, T. 2010. Local and global perspectives in the study of social and cultural identities. In S. Hales and T. Hodos (eds) *Material Culture and Social Identities in the Ancient World*, 3-31. Cambridge: Cambridge University Press.

Hogbin, H.I. 1935. Trading Expeditions in Northern New Guinea. *Oceania* 5(4): 375-407.

Hohmann-Vogrin, A. 2005. Space Syntax in Maya Architecture. In A. van Nes (ed.) *5th International Space Syntax Symposium Proceedings*, 279-292. West Lafayette and Ashland: Purdue University Press and AtlasBooks Distribution.

Holloway, R.R. 2005. Fortifications with towers in Bronze Age Sicily. In R. Gigli (ed.) *Megalai Nesoi. Studi dedicati a Giovanni Rizza per il suo ottantesimo compleanno*, 299-305. Catania: Consiglio Nazionale delle Ricerche IBAM.

Hopkins, M.R. 1987. Network Analysis of the Plans of Some Teotihuacán Apartment Compounds. *Environment and Planning B: Planning and Design* 14(4): 387-406.

Horden, P. and Purcell, N. 2000. *The Corrupting Sea: A Study of Mediterranean History*. Oxford: Blackwell.

Hussain, Z. 2016. Foreword. In C. Biagioli, M. De Chiara, E. Ferrari, A. Rana, S.A. Khan and M. Vidale, *Guide to the Kandak and Kotah Valleys. A field companion to Talking Stones*, i – iii. Lahore: Sang-e-Meel.

Iacono, F. 2013. Westernising LH IIIC. In M. E. Alberti and S. Sabatini (eds) *Exchange networks and local transformations: Interactions and local changes in Europe and the Mediterranean between the Bronze Age and the Iron Age*, 60-79. Oxford: Oxbow Books.

Iacono, F. 2015. Feasting at Roca: Cross-cultural encounters and society in the Southern Adriatic during the Late Bronze Age. *European Journal of Archaeology* 18: 259-281.

Iacono, F. 2016. From network to society: Pottery, style and hegemony in Bronze Age southern Italy. *Cambridge Archaeological Journal* 26(1): 121-40.

Iacono, F. 2017. The exception and the rule. Making sense of the diversity in patterns of Aegean interaction in Late Bronze Age Central Mediterranean. In A. Vlachopoulos, Y. Lolos, R. Laffineur, and M. Fotiadis (eds) *Hesperos. The Aegean seen from the west. Proceedings of the 16th international Aegean conference, University of Ioannina, Department of History and Archaeology, Unit of Archaeology and Art History, 18 – 21 May 2016*, 205-214. Leuven-Liège: Peeters.

Iacono, F. 2019. *The Archaeology of Late Bronze Age Interaction and Mobility at the Gates of Europe: People, Things and Networks Around the Southern Adriatic Sea*. London, UK: Bloomsbury Academic.

Irwin, G.J. 1978. The Development of Mailu as a Specialized Trading and Manufacturing Centre in Papuan Prehistory: The Causes and Implications. *Mankind* 11: 406-415.

Irwin, G.J. 1983. Kula and Trade in Massim Prehistory. In J. W. Leach, J. W. and E. Leach (eds) *The Kula – New Perspectives on Massim Exchange*, 29-72. Cambridge: Cambridge University Press.

Irwin, G.J. 1992. *The Prehistoric Exploration and Colonisation of the Pacific*. Cambridge: Cambridge University Press.

Jenkins, D. 2001. A Network Analysis of Inca Roads, Administrative Centers, and Storage Facilities. *Ethnohistory* 48: 655-687.

Jiang, B. 2009. Ranking Spaces for Predicting Human Movement in an Urban Environment. *International Journal of Geographical Information Science* 23(7): 823-837.

Jones, R.E., Levi, S. and Bettelli, M. 2005. Mycenaean pottery in the central Mediterranean: Imports, imitations and derivatives. In R. Laffineur and E. Greco (eds) *Emporia: Aegeans in the Central and Eastern Mediterranean, Proceedings of the 10th International Aegean Conference, Athens, Italian School of Archaeology, 14 – 18 April 2004*, 539-46. Liège and Austin, TX: Université de Liège, Histoire de l'Art et Archéologie de la Grèce Antique.

Jones, R.E., Levi, S., Bettelli, M. and Vagnetti, L. 2014. *Italo-Mycenaean Pottery: the Archaeological and Archaeometric Dimensions*. Rome: Incunabula Graeca CNR-ISMA.

Jones, S.G. and Fair, C.C. 2010. *Counterinsurgency in Pakistan*. Santa Monica, Ca: Rand.

Kaiser, A. 2011. *Roman Urban Street Networks*. New York: Routledge.

Kardulias, P.N. 2009. World-systems applications for understanding the Bronze Age in the eastern Mediterranean. In W. A. Parkinson and M. L. Galaty (eds) *Archaic State Interaction. The Eastern Mediterranean in the Bronze Age*, 53-80. Santa Fe: School for Advanced Research Press.

Kardulias, P.N. and Hall, T.D. 2008. Archaeology and World-Systems Analysis. *World Archaeology* 40(4): 572-583.

Kaufhold, K.H. 2001. Die Stadt als Verkehrsraum. In A. Niederstätter (ed.) *Stadt: Strom – Straße – Schiene: die Bedeutung des Verkehrs für die Genese der mitteleuropäischen Städtelandschaft*.Beiträge zur Geschichte der Städte Mitteleuropas, 27-53. Linz: Österreich. Arbeitskreis für Stadtgeschichtsforschung.

Khan, R. 2013. The reclamation of Gandhara cultural heritage. Its uses in present-day Khyber-Pakhtunkhwa. *Conservation Science in Cultural Heritage* 13: 259-270.

Killen, J.T. 1985. The Linear B tablets and the Mycenaean economy. In A. Davies, A. and Y. Duhoux (eds) *Linear B: a 1984 Survey*, 241-305. Louvain: BCILL.

Kirch, P.V. 1991. Prehistoric Exchange in Western Melanesia. *Annual Review of Anthropology* 20: 141-165.

Knappett, C. (ed.) 2013. *Network Analysis in Archaeology: New Approaches to Regional Interaction*. Oxford: Oxford University Press.

Knappett, C. 2014. What are Social Network Perspectives in Archaeology? *Archaeological Review from Cambridge* 29(1): 179-84.

Knappett, C. 2017. Globalization, Connectivities and Networks. An Archaeological Perspective. In T. Hodos (ed.) *The Routledge Handbook of Archaeology and Globalization*, 29-41. London and New York; Routledge.

Knappett, C., Evans, T. and Rivers, R. 2008. Modelling Maritime Interaction in the Aegean Bronze Age. *Antiquity* 82: 1009-1024.

Knappett, C. and Nikolakopoulou, I. 2015. Inside Out? Materiality and Connectivity in the Aegean Archipelago. In A. B. Knapp and P. van Dommelen (eds) *Cambridge Handbook of the Bronze Age-Iron Age Mediterranean World*, 25-39. Cambridge: University Press Cambridge.

Koch, D., Marcus, L. and Steen, J. (eds) 2009. *Proceedings of the 7th International Space Syntax Symposium*. Stockholm: KTH.

Kristiansen, K. 1998. The Emergence of the European World System in the Bronze Age: Divergence, Convergence and Social Evolution During the First and Second Millennia. In K. Kristiansen and M. Rowlands (eds) *Social Transformations in Archaeology: Global and Local Perspectives*, 287-324. London: Routledge.

La Rosa, V.P. 2000. Riconsiderazioni sulla Media Tarda Età del Bronzo nella Media Valle del Platani. *Quaderni dell'Istituto di Archeologia della Facoltà di Lettere e Filosofia dell'Università di Messina* 1: 125-138.

La Rosa, V.P. 2004. Le presenze Micenee nel territorio Siracusano: per una storia del problema. In V. La Rosa (ed.) *Le Presenze Micenee nel Territorio Siracusano*, 9-44. Catania: Centro di Archeologia Cretese.

LaCapra, D. 2001. *Writing History, Writing Trauma*. Baltimore: John Hopkins University Press.

Latour, B. 2007. *Reassembling the Social: An Introduction to Actor-Network-Theory*. Oxford: Oxford University Press.

Lay, M. 1992. *Ways of the World: A History of the World's Roads and of the Vehicles that Used Them*. New Jersey: Piscataway.

Leach, J.W. and Leach, E. 1983. *The Kula: New Perspectives on Massim Exchange*. Cambridge: Cambridge University Press.

Lefebvre, H. 2009. *The Production of Space*. Malden, MA; Oxford: Blackwell.

Leighton, R. 1999. *Sicily before History. An archaeological survey from the Palaeolithic to the Iron Age*. London: Duckworth.

Leskovec, J. and Horvitz, E. 2014. Geospatial Structure of a Planetary-Scale Social Network. *IEEE Transactions on Computational Social Systems* 1(3): 156-163.

Letesson, Q. 2014. From Building to Architecture: The Rise of Configurational Thinking in Bronze Age Crete. In E. Paliou, U. Lieberwirth and S. Polla (eds) *Spatial Analysis and Social Spaces*, 49-90. Berlin: De Gruyter

Lilley, I. 1986. *Prehistoric Exchange in the Vitiaz Strait, Papua New Guinea*. Unpublished PhD dissertation. Canberra: Australian National University.

Lipset, D. 1985. Seafaring Sepiks: Ecology, Warfare, and Prestige in Murik Trade. *Research in Economic Anthropology* 7: 67-94.

Liverani, M. 2002. The Great Powers' Club. In R. Cohen and R. Westbrook (eds) *Amarna Diplomacy: The Beginnings of International Relations*, 15-27. Baltimore: Johns Hopkins University Press.

Lorenz, A. 2010. *Stadtarchäologie im Nürnberger Rotgerberviertel: Die Ausgrabungen in der Vorderen Ledergasse 1989*. Büchenbach: Faustus.

Lo Schiavo F. 2006. Ipotesi sulla circolazione dei metalli nel Mediterraneo centrale, in *Atti XXXIX Riunione Scientifica IIPP, Firenze*, 1319-1337. Istituto di Preistoria e Protostoria.

Low, S.M. 1996. Spatializing Culture: The Social Production and Social Construction of Public Space in Costa Rica. *American Ethnologist* 23(4): 861-79.

Löw, M. 2015. *Raumsoziologie* 8. Auflage. Frankfurt am Main: Suhrkamp.

Luick, L. 2016: Süßer die Glocken nie klingen Das Potential akustischer Untersuchungen von Kirchenglocken am Beispiel der St.-Katharinen-Glocke. *Arkæologi i Slesvig/Archäologie in Schleswig* 16: 85-99.

Lukács, G. 1971. *History and Class Consciousness: Studies in Marxist Dialectics*. London: Merlin Press.

Luxemburg, R. 2003. *The Accumulation of Capital*. London; New York: Routledge.

Lynch, K. 1960. *The Image of the City*. Cambridge Mass.: MIT Press.

Malkin, I. 2011. *A Small Greek World: Networks in the ancient Mediterranean*. Oxford: Oxford University Press.

Mammone, A. 2006. A Daily Revision of the Past: Fascism, Anti-Fascism, and Memory in Contemporary Italy. *Modern Italy* 11: 211-226.

Mannino, G. 1992. Ustica. *Κώκαλος* 26-27: 823-828.

Maran, J. and Stockhammer, P.W. 2012. Introduction Materiality and Social Practice. In J. Maran and P.W. Stockhammer (eds) *Transformative Capacities and Intercultural Encounters*, 1-3. Oxford: Oxbow Books.

Marazzi, M. 2003. The Mycenaeans in the Western Mediterranean (17th – 13th c. BC). In N. S. Stampolidis (ed.) *Ploes. Sea routes from Sidon to Huelva. Catalogo della Mostra, Atene 2003*, 108-115. Athens: Museum of Cycladic Art and Hellenic Ministry of Culture.

Marino, T. 2015. Aspetti e fasi del processo formativo delle città in Etruria meridionale costiera. Le città visibili. In M. Rendeli (ed.) *Archeologia dei processi di formazione urbana I. Penisola Italiana e Sardegna*, 97-141. Roma: Officina Etruscologia.

Markovsky, B., Skvoretz, J., D, W., Lovaglia, M.J. and Erger, J. 1993. The Seeds of Weak Power: An Extension of Network Exchange Theory. *American Sociological Review* 58(2): 197 – 209.

Marx, K. 1976. *Capital: A Critique of Political Economy*. Vol. 1. London; New York, N.Y.: Penguin Books in association with New Left Review.

Marx, K. 1992. *Capital: A Critique of Political Economy*. Vol. 2. London; New York, N.Y.: Penguin Books in association with New Left Review.

Mathieu, J.R. 1999. New Methods on Old Castles: Generating New Ways of Seeing. *Medieval Archaeology* (43): 115-142.

Mattingly, D.J. 1997. Introduction. Dialogues of Power and Experience in the Roman Empire. In D.J. Mattingly (ed.) *Dialogues in Roman Imperialism. Power, Discourse and Discrepant Experience in the Roman Empire*, 7 – 24. Portsmouth, Rhode Island.

Mauss, M. 1966. *The Gift: Forms and Functions of Exchange in Archaic Societies*. London: Routledge and Kegan Paul.

Mazzocchi, F. 2015. Could Big Data be the End of Theory in Science? *EMBO Reports* 16(19). Available at: https://doi.org/10.1252/embr.201541001.

McPherson, M., Smith-Lovin, L. and Cook, J. 2001. Birds of a Feather: Homophily in Social Networks. *Annual Review of Sociology* 27: 415-444.

Meckseper, C. 2002. Raumdifferenzierung im hochmittelalterlichen Burgenbau Mitteleuropas. *Château Gaillard* (20): 163-171.

Meillassoux, C. 1975. *Femmes, Greniers et Capitaux*. Paris: F. Maspero.

Mermet, E. and Robert, S. 2014. Exploring Network Structural Properties with the GeoGraphLab GIS Solution [Symposium Paris 2014]. Available at: http://geographlab.free.fr/caa2014/.

Mialanes, J., David, B., Ford, A., Richards, T., McNiven, I.J., Summerhayes, G.R. and Leavesley, M. 2016. Imported obsidian at Caution Bay, south coast of Papua New Guinea: cessation of long distance procurement c. 1,900 Cal BP. *Australian Archaeology* 82(3): 248-262.

Mihajlović, V.D. 2019. Critique of Romanization in Classical Archaeology. In C. Smith (ed.) *Encyclopedia of Global Archaeology*, 1-11. Springer International Publishing.

Militello, P. 2005. Mycenaean Palaces and western Trade: A complex Relationship. In R. Laffineur and E. Greco (eds) *Emporia: Aegeans in the Central and Eastern Mediterranean, Proceedings of the 10th International Aegean Conference, Athens, Italian School of Archaeology, 14 – 18 April 2004*, 585-98. Liège and Austin, TX: Université de Liège, Histoire de l'Art et Archéologie de la Grèce Antique.

Mills, B.J. 2017. Social Network Analysis in Archaeology. *Annual Review of Anthropology* 46(1): 379-97.

Mitchell, P. 2015. Raum und Repräsentation in der Gozzoburg. In C. Schmid (ed) *Raumstrukturen und Raumausstattung auf Burgen in Mittelalter und Früher Neuzeit*. Interdisziplinäre Beiträge zu Mittelalter und Früher Neuzeit, 279-308. Heidelberg: Winter.

Mogetta, M. 2014. Latium Vetus-Latium Adjectum. In C. Smith (ed.) *Encyclopedia of Global Archaeology*, 4450-4459. New York: Springer International Publishing.

Moran, W.L. 1992. *The Amarna Letters*. Baltimore, MD: Johns Hopkins University Press.

Morris, I. 2003. Mediterraneanization. *Mediterranean Historical Review* 18(2): 30-55.

Morton, S.G., Peuramaki-Brown, M.M., Dawson, P.C. and Seibert, J.D. 2012. Civic and Household Community Relationships at Teotihuacan, Mexico: A Space Syntax Approach. *Cambridge Archaeological Journal* 22(03): 387-400.

Nakoinz, O. 2012a. Ausgewählte Parameter der Lage von Wegen und Monumenten als Proxy für soziale Prozesse prähistorischer Gesellschaften. In M. Hinz and J. Müller (eds) *Siedlung, Grabenwerk, Großsteingrab. Studien zu Gesellschaft, Wirtschaft und Umwelt der Trichterbechergruppen im nördlichen Mitteleuropa. Frühe Monumentalität und soziale Differenzierung 2*, 445-456. Bonn; Habelt.

Nakoinz, O. 2012b. Verkehrswege der älteren Eisenzeit in Südwestdeutschland. In C. Tappert, C. Later, J. Fries-Knoblach, P. C. Ramsl, P. Trebsche, S. Wefers, and J. Wiethold (eds) *Wege und Transport. Beiträge Sitzung der AG Eisenzeit während der 80. Verbandstagung des West- und Süddeutschen Verbandes für Altertumsforschung e. V. in Nürnberg 2010. Beiträge zur Ur- und Frühgeschichte Mitteleuropas* 69, 73-82. Langenweissbach: Beier & Beran.

Nakoinz, O. 2013a. *Archäologische Kulturgeographie der ältereisenzeitlichen Zentralorte Südwestdeutschlands*. Bonn: Universitätsforsch. prähist. Arch. 224.

Nakoinz, O. 2013b. Models of Interaction and Economical Archaeology. *Metalla* 20(2): 107-115.

Nakoinz, O. 2013c. Räumliche Interaktionsmodelle. *Prähistorische Zeitschrifte* 88: 226-257.

Nakoinz, O. 2013d. *Archäologische Kulturgeographie der ältereisenzeitlichen Zentralorte Südwestdeutschlands: Zugl.: Kiel, Univ., Habil.-Schr., 2010*. Bonn: Habelt.

Nakoinz, O., Bilger, M. and Matzig, D. 2020. Urbanity as a Process and the Role of Relative Network Properties – A Case Study from the Early Iron Age. In F. Fulminante, L. Prignano and R.J. Rivers (eds) *Frontiers of Digital Humanities 7:2*. doi: 10.3389/fdigh.2020.00002.

Netto, V.M. 2016. 'What is Space Syntax not?' Reflections on Space Syntax as Sociospatial Theory. *URBAN DESIGN International* 21(1): 25-40.

Newman, M.E.J. and Park, J. 2003. Why Social Networks are Different from other Types of Networks. *Physical Review E* 68(3Pt2).

Niederstätter, A. (ed.) 2001. *Stadt: Strom – Straße – Schiene: Die Bedeutung des Verkehrs für die Genese der mitteleuropäischen Städtelandschaft*. Linz: Österreich. Arbeitskreis für Stadtgeschichtsforschung.

Ollman, B. 2003. *Dance of the Dialectic: Steps in Marx's Method*. Urbana: University of Illinois Press.

Onnela J.-P., Arbesman, S., González, M.C., Barabási, A.L. and Christakis, N.A. 2011. Geographic Constraints on Social Network Groups. *PLoS One*. 2011;6(4):e16939. doi:10.1371/journal.pone.0016939.

Orengo, H.A. and Livarda, A. 2016. The Seeds of Commerce: A Network Analysis-Based Approach to the Romano-British Transport System. *Journal of Archaeological Science* 66: 21-35.

Östborn, P. and Gerding, H. 2014. Network Analysis of Archaeological Data: A Systematic Approach. *Journal of Archaeological Science* 46: 75-88.

Ouzman, S. 2006. The Beauty of Letting Go. Fragmentary Museums and Archaeologies of Archive. In C. Gosden, E. Edwards, and R. Phillips (eds) *Sensible Objects: Museums, Colonialism and the Senses*, 269-301. Oxford: Berg.

Pacciarelli, M. 2001. *Dal Villaggio alla Città. La Svolta Proto-Urbana del 1000 A.C. nell'italia Tirrenica*. Florence: All'Insegna del Giglio.

Pacciarelli, M. 2010. Forme di complessità sociale nelle comunità protourbane dell'Etruria meridionale. In P. Fontaine (ed.) *L'Étrurie et l'Ombrie avant Rome. Cité et Territoire. Actes du Colloque International Louvain-la-Neuve 2004*, 17-33. Brüssel and Rome: Institut Historique Belge de Rome.

Pacciarelli, M. 2017. The Transition from Villages Communities to Proto-Urban Societies. In A. B. Naso (ed.) *Etruscology*, 561-581. Boston/Berlin: de Gruyter.

Palio, O. 2004. Proiezioni esterne e dinamiche interne nell'area siracusana fra il Bronzo Antico e Medio. In V. La Rosa (ed.) *Le presenze micenee nel territorio* siracusano. Atti del I Simposio Siracusano di Preistoria Siciliana, 73-98. Catania: Centro di Archeologia Cretese.

Paliou, E. 2014. Visibility Analysis in 3D Spaces: A New Dimension to the Understanding of Social Space. In E. Paliou, U. Lieberwirth and S. Polla (eds) *Spatial Analysis and Social Spaces*, 91-113. Berlin: De Gruyter.

Paliou, E. and Bevan, A. 2016. Evolving Settlement Patterns, Spatial Interaction and the Socio-Political Organisation of Late Prepalatial South-Central Crete. *Journal of Anthropological Archaeology* 42: 184-197.

Palmisano, A. 2017. Confronting Scales of Settlement Hierarchy in State-Level Societies: Upper Mesopotamia and Central Anatolia in the Middle Bronze Age. *Journal of Archaeological Science: Reports* 14: 220-240.

Papadopoulos, C. and Earl, G. 2014. Formal Three-Dimensional Computational Analyses of Archaeological Spaces. In E. Paliou, U. Lieberwirth and S. Polla (eds) *Spatial Analysis and Social Spaces*, 135-166. Berlin: De Gruyter.

Parry, R. 2007. *Recoding the Museum: Digital Heritage and the Technologies of Change*. London: Routledge.

Paterson, A. 2011. *A Millennium of Cultural Contact*. Walnut Creek (CA): Left Coast Press.

Pauketat, T.R. 1997. *Chiefdoms and Other Archaeological Delusions*. Plymouth: AltaMira Press.

Pauketat, T.R. 2008. The Grounds for Agency in Southwest Archaeology. In M. D. Varien and J. M. Potter (eds) *The Social Construction of Communities: Agency, Structure, and Identity in the Prehispanic Southwest*, 233-249. Plymouth: AltaMira Press.

Pavone, C. 1991 (2014) *Una Guerra Civile. Saggio Storico sulla Moralità della Resistenza*. Turin: Bollati Boringhieri.

Peinetti, A., Magrì, A., Wattez, J., Tusa, S., Lefèvre, D. 2015. *Spatial geoarchaeology at the Bronze Age village of Mursia (Pantelleria, Italy): Activity areas in a polyfunctional room*. Conference poster presented at the EAA 21st Annual Meeting in Glasgow.

Penn, A., Hillier, B., Banister, D. and Xu, J. 1998. Configurational Modelling of Urban Movement Networks. *Environment and Planning B: Planning and Design* 25(1): 59-84.

Peponis, J., Wineman, J. and Bafna, S. (eds) 2001. *Proceedings of the 3rd International Space Syntax Symposium.* Atlanta: Ann Arbor.

Perkins, T.A., Garcia, A.J., Paz-Soldán, V.A., Stoddard, S.T., Reiner, R.C. Robert, Vazquez-Prokopec, G., Bisanzio, D., Morrison, A.C., Halsey, E.S., Kochel, T.J., Smith, D.L., Kitron, U., Scott, T.W. and Tatem, A.J. 2014. Theory and Data for Simulating Fine-Scale Human Movement in an Urban Environment. *Journal of the Royal Society – Interface* 11(99): 1120140642.

Pezzino, P. 2005. The Italian Resistance between History and Memory. *Journal of Modern Italian Studies* 10(4): 396 – 412.

Pinder, D. 1979. The Nearest-Neighbor Statistic: Archaeological Application and New Development. *American Antiquity* 44(3): 430-445.

Pizziolo, G. De Silva, M., Volante, N. and Cristoferi, D. 2016. *Transumanza e Territorio in Toscana: Percorsi e Pascoli dalla Protostoria all'Età contemporanea. La Strutturazione del Sistema Informativo e le Attività di Ricognizione Archeologica.* Chronique des activités archéologiques de l'École Française de Rome. https://doi.org/10.4000/cefr.1836.

Pfinzing, P. 1588. *Grundriss der Stadt Nürnberg: Pfinzing Atlas, Blatt 8.* Available at: https://commons.wikimedia.org/wiki/File:Pfinzing_N%C3%BCrnberg_Grundriss.jpg?uselang=de.

Portelli, A. 2003. The massacre at the Fosse Ardeatine: History, Myth, Ritual and Symbol. In K. Hodgkin and S. Radstone (eds) *Contested Pasts: the Politics of Memory*, 30-40. London

Potter, T.W. 1979. *The Changing Landscape of South Etruria.* London: Paul Elek.

Prag, J.R.W. and Quinn, J.C. (eds) 2013 *The Hellenistic West: Rethinking the Ancient Mediterranean.* Cambridge: Cambridge University Press.

Prey, R. 2012. The Network's Blindspot: Exclusion, Exploitation and Marx's Process-Relational Ontology. *TripleC: Communication, Capitalism and Critique. Open Access Journal for a Global Sustainable Information Society* 10(2): 253-273.

Prignano, L., Morer, I., Lozano, S., Perez, J., Fulminante, F., Dìaz-Guilera, A. 2017. The Weird, Wired Past. The Challenges of Applying Network Science to Archaeology and Ancient History. In J. R. Rodríguez (ed.) *Economía Romana: Nuevas Perspectivas*, 125 – 48. Barcelona: Universitat de Barcelona Edicions.

Prignano, L., Morer. I., Lozano, S., Perez, J., Fulminante, F. and Dìaz-Guilera, A. 2019. Modelling Terrestrial Route Networks to Understand Inter-Polity Interactions. A Case-Study from Southern Etruria. *Journal of Archaeological Science* 105: 46-58.

Pulak, C. 2001. The Cargo of the Uluburun Ship and Evidence for Trade with the Aegean and beyond. In L. Bonfante and V. Karageorghis (eds) *Italy and Cyprus in Antiquity 1500 – 450 BC, Proceedings of an International Symposium held at the Italian Academy for Advanced Studies in America at Columbia University, 16 – 18 November 2000*, 13-60. Nicosia: Severis Foundation.

Purcell, N. 1990. The Creation of Provincial Landscape: The Roman Impact on Cisalpine Gaul. In T. F. C. Blagg and M. Millett (eds) *The Early Roman Empire in the West*, 7 – 29. Oxford: Oxbow Books.

Qaiser, F. 2009. Archbishop of Lahore: Sharia in the Swat Valley is contrary to Pakistan's founding principles". *AsiaNews.it* 21 April 2009. Last accessed on 27/7/2016.

Radivojević, M. and Grujić, J. 2018. Community Structure of Copper Supply Networks in the Prehistoric Balkans: An Independent Evaluation of the Archaeological Record from the 7th to the 4th millennium BC. *Journal of Complex Networks* 6(1): 106-24.

Rapoport, A. 1982. *The Meaning of the Built Environment: A Nonverbal Communication Approach* 1. print. Thousand Oaks Calif. u.a.: Sage Publ.

Rasmussen, T. 2005. Urbanization in Etruria. In R. Osborne and B. Cunliffe (eds) *Mediterranean Urbanization 800 – 600 BC*, 91 – 113. Oxford: Oxford University Press.

Ratti, C. 2004. Space Syntax: Some Inconsistencies. *Environment and Planning B: Planning and Design* 31(4): 487-499.

Rautman, A. 1993. Resource Variability, Risk, and the Structure of Social Networks: An Example from the Prehistoric Southwest. *American Antiquity* 58(3): 403 – 424.

Reckwitz, A. 2016. *Kreativität und soziale Praxis: Studien zur Sozial- und Gesellschaftstheorie*. Transcript Verlag. Available at: http://dx.doi.org/10.14361/9783839433454.

Rendeli, M. 1993. *Città Aperte. Ambiente e Paesaggio Rurale Organizzato nell'Etruria Meridionale Costiera durante l'Età Orientalizzante e Arcaica*. Rome: Gruppo Editoriale Internazionale.

Renfrew, A.C. 1999. The Loom of Language and the Versailles Effect. In P.P. Betancourt, V. Karagheorghis, R. Laffineur, and W.D. Niemeier (eds) *MELETEMATA. Studies in Aegean Archaeology Presented to Malcolm H. Wiener as He Enters his 65th Year*, 711-719. Aegaeum, Liège : Austin: Université de Liège and University of Texas at Austin.

Renfrew, C. 1986. Interazione fra comunità paritarie e formazione dello stato. *Dialoghi di Archeologia* 3(4): 27 – 33.

Richardson, A. 2003. Gender and Space in English Royal Palaces c. 1160-c. 1547: A Study in Access Analysis and Imagery. *Medieval Archaeology* 47(1): 131-165.

Ricoeur, P. 1981. *Memory, History, Forgetting*. Chicago: University of Chicago Press.

Riva, C. 2010. *The Urbanisation of Etruria: Funerary Practices and Social Change, 700-600 BC*. Cambridge: Cambridge University Press.

Rizio, A. 2005. Vivara: An "International" port in the Bronze Age Mediterranean. In R. Laffineur and E. Greco (eds) *Emporia: Aegeans in the Central and Eastern Mediterranean*, 609-623. Liège and Austin: Université de Liège, Histoire de l'Art et Archéologie de la Grèce Antique.

Robb, J. and Farr, H. 2005. Substances in Motion: Neolithic Mediterranean Trade. In E. Blake and A. B. Knapp (eds) *The Archaeology of Mediterranean Prehistory*, 24-45. Oxford; Malden MA: Blackwell.

Robb, M.H. 2007. *The Spatial Logic of Zacuala, Teotihuacan*. Proceedings, 6th International Space Syntax Symposium, İstanbul, 2007, published online: http://www.spacesyntaxistanbul.itu.edu.tr/papers/longpapers/062%20-%20Robb.pdf.

Roth, R.E. 2007. *Styling Romanisation: Pottery and Society in Central Italy*. Cambridge; New York: Cambridge University Press.

Rowlands M.J. and Gledhill J. 1998. Materialism and multilinear evolution. In K. Kristiansen and M.J. Rowlands (eds) *Social Transformations in Archaeology: Global and Local Perspectives*, 36-44. London: Routledge.

Russell, A. 2017. Sicily without Mycenae: A cross-cultural consumption analysis of connectivity in the Bronze Age Central Mediterranean. *Journal of Mediterranean Archaeology* 30(1): 59-83.

Russell, A. and Knapp, B.A. 2017. Sardinia and Cyprus: An alternative view on Cypriotes in the central Mediterranean. *Papers of the British School at Rome* 85: 1-35.

Ruyle, E.E. 1973. Slavery, Surplus, and Stratification on the Northwest Coast: The Ethnoenergetics of an Incipient Stratification System. *Current Anthropology* 14(5): 603-31.

Sahlins, M. 1995. *How 'Natives' Think: About Captain Cook, For Example*. Chicago: University of Chicago Press.

Saitta, D.J. 2005. Marxism, Tribal Society, and the Dual Nature of Archaeology. *Rethinking Marxism* 17(3): 385-397.

Saltini Semerari, G. 2016. Towards an Archaeology of Disentanglement. *Journal of Archaeological Method and Theory* 24(2): 542-578.

Schiappelli, A. 2008. *Sviluppo Storico della Teverina*. Florence: All'Insegna del Giglio.

Schiermeier, F. (ed.) 2006. *Stadtatlas Nürnberg: Karten und Modelle von 1492 bis heute*. München: Schiermeier.

Schmid, C., Schichta, G., Kühtreiber, T. and Holzner-Tobisch, K. (eds) 2015. *Raumstrukturen und Raumausstattung auf Burgen in Mittelalter und Früher Neuzeit*. Heidelberg: Winter.

Schortman, E.M. 1989. Interregional Interaction in Prehistory: The Need for a New Perspective. *American Antiquity* 54(1): 52-65.

Schroder, C., Mackaness, W. and Reitsma, F.E. 2007. *Quantifying Urban Visibility Using 3D Space Syntax*. Geographic Information Science Research Conference (GISRUK), Maynooth, Ireland, 11 – 13th April 2007. Published online: http://www.geos.ed.ac.uk/homes/wam/SchroderMack2007.pdf

Schwesinger, S. 2017. *Auralisation archäologischer Räume. Von 3D-Modellen zur Rekonstruktion auditiver Erfahrung in der Antike*. Available at: https://prezi.com/dy60gjdeasje/auralisation-archaeologischer-raume/.

Scott, J. 2010. Social Network Analysis: Developments, Advances, and Prospects. *Social Network Analysis and Mining* 1(1): 21-26.

Secondo, M., Vandini, M., Fiori, C. and Cattani, M. 2011. Caratterizzazione mineralogico-petrografica di reperti ceramici provenienti dal settore B del villaggio dell'età del Bronzo di Mursia. In S. Gualtieri, E. Starnini, R. Cabella, C. Capelli and B. Fabbri (eds) *La ceramica e il mare. Il contributo dell'archeometria allo studio della circolazione dei prodotti nel Mediterraneo*, 29-39. Roma: Aracne.

Service, E.R. 1962. *Primitive Social Organization: An Evolutionary Perspective*. New York: Random House.

Shanks, M. and Tilley, C.Y. 1987. *Social Theory and Archaeology*. University of New Mexico Press.

Sherlock, R. 2010. Changing Perceptions: Spatial Analysis and the Study of the Irish Tower House. *Château Gaillard* 24: 239-250.

Sherratt, A. 1993a. What would a Bronze Age World System look like? Relations between temperate Europe and the Mediterranean in later prehistory. *Journal of European Archaeology* 1(2): 1-57.

Sherratt, A. 1993b. Who are you calling peripheral? Dependence and independence in European Prehistory. In C. Scarre and F. Healy (eds) *Trade and Exchange in Prehistoric Europe*, 245-55. Oxford: Oxbow Books.

Sherratt, A. 1994. Core, Periphery, and Margin. In C. Mathers and S. Stoddart (eds) *Development and decline in the Mediterranean Bronze Age*, 335-345. Sheffield: J.R. Collis.

Sherratt, S. 2017. A globalizing Bronze and Iron Age Mediterranean. In T. Hodos (ed.) *The Routledge Handbook of Archaeology and Globalization*, 602-17. London: Routledge.

Sherratt, A. and Sherratt, S. 1989. Small worlds: Interaction and identity in the ancient Mediterranean. In E. H. Cline and D. Harris-Cline (eds) *The Aegean and the Orient in the Second Millennium: Proceedings of the 50th Anniversary Symposium Cincinnati, 18-20 April 1997*, 329-343. Texas, Liège: Histoire de l'Art et Archéologie de la Grèce Antique, University of Texas at Austin.

Sherratt, A. and Sherratt, S. 1991. From Luxuries to Commodities: The nature of Mediterranean Bronze Age Trading Systems. In N. H. Gale (ed.) *Bronze Age Trade in the Mediterranean*, 351-386. Jonsered: Paul Åströms Förlag.

Shi, X., Adamic, L.A. and Strauss, M.J. 2007. Networks of Strong Ties. *Physica A* 378: 33-47.

Silvestru, C. 2014. The Leveling of the High Medieval Viennese City Moat. A Space Syntax Perspective. In W. Börner and S. Uhlirz (eds) *Proceedings of the 18th International Conference on Cultural Heritage and New Technologies*. Museen der Stadt – Stadtarchäologie (Hrsg./Verleger), 2013, Wien. Published online: http://www.chnt.at/proceedings-chnt-18/

Skoglund, P., Posth, C., Kendra, S., Spriggs, M., Valentin, F., Bedford, S., Clark, G.R., Reepmeyer, C., Petchey, F., Fernandes, D., Fu, Q., Harney, E. Lipson, M., Mallick, S., Novak, M., Rohland, N., Stewardson, K., Abdullah, S., Cox, M.P., Friedlaender, F., Friedlaender, J., Kivisild, T., Koki, G., Kusuma, P., Merriwether, D.A., Ricaut, F.-X., Wee, J.T.S., Patterson, N., Krause, J., Pinhasi, R. and D. Reich. 2016. Genomic insights into the peopling of the southwest Pacific. *Nature* 538: 510-513.

Smith, C.J. 1996. *Early Rome and Latium. Economy and Society c.1000 to 500 BC.* Oxford: Clarendon Press.

Smith, C.J. 2007. Latium and the Latins: the Hinterland of Rome. In G. Bradley, E. Isayev and C. Riva (eds) *Ancient Italy. Regions without Boundaries*, 161-179. Exeter: Exeter University Press.

Smith, E.A., Borgerhoff Mulder, M., Bowles, S., Gurven, M., Hertz, T. and Shenket, M.K. 2010. Production systems, inheritance, and inequality in premodern societies: Conclusions. *Current Anthropology* 51(1): 85-94.

Smith, L.M. 2005. Network, Territories, and the Cartography of Ancient States. *Annals of the Associations of American Geographers* 95(4): 832-849.

Soares, P., Rito, T., Trejaut, J., Mormina, M., Hill, C., Tinkler-Hundal, E., Braid, M., Clarke, D.J., Loo, J-H., Thomson, N., Denham, T., Donohue, M. Macaulay, V., Lin, M., Oppenheimer, S. and Richards, M.B. 2011. Ancient Voyaging and Polynesian Origins. *The American Journal of Human Genetics* 88: 239-247.

Soja, E. 2001. In Different Spaces. Interpreting the Spatial Organization of Societies. In J. Peponis, J. Wineman and S. Bafna (eds) *Proceedings of the 3rd International Space Syntax Symposium*, 1-7. Atlanta.

Sparrowe, R., Liden, R., Wayne, S. and Kraimer, M. 2001. Social Networks and the Performance of Individuals and Groups. *Academy of Management Journal* 44(2): 316-325.

Spatafora, F. 2009. Spazio Abitativo e Architettura Domestica negli Insediamenti Indigeni della Sicilia Occidentale. In M. C. Belarte (ed.) *L'espai domèstic i l'organització de la societat a la protohistòria de la Mediterrània occidental (Ier millenni aC). Actes de la IV Reunió Internacional d'Arqueologia de Calafell (Calafell, Tarragona, 6 al 9 de març de 2007)*, 363-377. Barcelona: Area d'Arqueologia-Universitat de Barcelona, Institut Català d'Arqueologia Clàssica.

Spatafora, F. 2016. Tra Mare e Terra: La Preistoria di Ustica e il Villaggio del Faraglione. *Scienze dell'Antichità* 22(2): 315-326.

Specht, J., Denham, T., Goff, J. and Terrell, J.E. 2014. Deconstructing the Lapita cultural complex in the Bismarck Archipelago. *Journal of Archaeological Research* 22: 89-140.

Stavroulaki, G. and Peponis, J. 2005. Seen in a Different Light. Icons in Byzantine Museums and Curches. In A. van Nes (ed.) *5th International Space Syntax Symposium Proceedings*, 251-263. West Lafayette and Ashland: Purdue University Press and Atlas-Books Distribution.

Stein, G. 2002. Colonies without Colonialism: A Trade Diaspora Model of 4th Millennium BC Mesopotamian Enclaves in Anatolia. In C. Lyons and J. Papadopoulos (eds) *The Archaeology of Colonialism*, 26-64. Los Angeles: J. Paul Getty Museum Publications.

Stockhammer, P.W. and Hahn, H.P. (eds) 2015. *Lost in Things – Fragen an die Welt des Materiellen*. Tübingen: Waxmann.

Stoddart, S.K. 2009. *Historical Dictionary of the Etruscans*. Plymouth: Scarecrow Press.

Stoddart, S.K. 2016. Power and Place in Etruria. In M. Fernandez-Götz and D. Krausse (eds) *Eurasia at the Dawn of History: Urbanization and Social Change*, 304-318. Cambridge: Cambridge University Press.

Stoddart, S.K., Palmisano, A., Redhouse, D., Barker, G., di Paola, G., Motta, L., Rasmussen, T., Samuels, T. and Witcher, R. 2020. Patterns of Etruscan Urbanism. *Frontiers of Digital Humanities* 7:1. doi: 10.3389/fdigh.2020.00001

Stoddart, S.K. 2020. *Power and Place in Etruria. The Spatial Dynamics of a Mediterranean Civilisation. 1200 – 500 BC*. Cambridge: Cambridge University Press.

Stoddart, S.K. and Spivey, N. 1990. *Etruscan Italy. An Archaeological History*. London: B.T. Batsford.

Stöger, H. 2008. Roman Ostia: Space Syntax and the Domestication of Space. In A. Posluschny, K. Lambers and I. Herzog (eds) *Layers of Perception*. Kolloquien zur Vor- und Frühgeschichte, 322-327. Bonn: Habelt.

Stöger, H. 2009. Clubs and Lounges at Roman Ostia: The Spatial Organisation of a Boomtown Phenomenon (Space Syntax Applied to the Study of Second Century AD 'Guild Buildings' at a Roman Port Town). In D. Koch, L. Marcus and J. Steen (eds) *Proceedings of the 7th International Space Syntax Symposium*. TRITA-ARK-Forsknings-publikation, 1-12. Stockholm: KTH. Available at: http://hdl.handle.net/1887/14297.

Stöger, H. 2011. *Rethinking Ostia: A Spatial Enquiry into the Urban Society of Rome's Imperial Port-Town: Zugl.: Leiden, Univ., Diss., 2011*. Leiden: Leiden Univ. Press. Available at: http://hdl.handle.net/1887/18192.

Summerhayes, G.R. 2004. The Nature of Prehistoric Obsidian Importation to Anir and the Development of a 3,000 Year Regional Picture of Obsidian Exchange within the Bismarck Archipelago, Papua New Guinea. *Records of the Australian Museum Supplement* 29: 145-156.

Summerhayes, G.R. 2009. Obsidian Network Patterns in Melanesia. Sources, Characterisation and Distribution. *IPPA Bulletin* 29: 109-124.

Summerhayes, G.R., Field, J.H., Shaw, B. and Gaffney, D. 2017. The Archaeology of Forest Exploitation and Change in the Tropics during the Pleistocene: The Case of Northern Sahul (Pleistocene New Guinea). *Quaternary International* 448: 14-30.

Swadling, P. 2004. Stone Mortar and Pestle Distribution in New Britain Revisited. *Records of the Australian Museum* Supplement 29: 157-161.

Szabó, K. and O'Connor, S. 2004. Migration and Complexity in Holocene Island Southeast Asia. *World Archaeology* 36(4): 621-628.

Tanasi, D. 2004. Per un riesame degli elementi di tipo miceneo nella cultura di Pantalica Nord. In V. La Rosa (ed.) *Le presenze micenee nel territorio siracusano. Atti del Primo simposio* siracusano di preistoria siciliana (Siracusa 15-16 dicembre 2003), 337 – 83. Catania: Centro di Archeologia Cretese.

Tanasi, D. 2005. Mycenaean pottery imports and local imitations: Sicily vs Southern Italy. In R. Laffineur and E. Greco (eds) *Emporia: Aegeans in the Central and Eastern Mediterranean, Proceedings of the 10th International Aegean Conference, Athens, Italian School of Archaeology, 14 – 18 April 2004*, 561-569. Liège and Austin: Université de Liège, Histoire de l'Art et Archéologie de la Grèce Antique.

Tanasi, D. 2008. *La Sicilia e l'arcipelago maltese nell'età del Bronzo Medio*. Palermo: Progetto KASA, Officina di Studi Medievali.

Tanasi, D. 2009. Sicily at the end of the Bronze Age: 'Catching the Echo'. In C. Bachhuber and R. Gareth Roberts (eds) *Forces of Transformation. The End of the Bronze Age in the Mediterranean*, 51-58. Oxford: Oxbow Books.

Tanasi, D. 2015. Borġ-in-Nadur pottery abroad: a report from the Sicilian necropoleis of Thapsos and Matrensa. In D. Tanasi and N. Vella (eds) *The Late Prehistory of Malta: Essays on Borġ-in-Nadur and other sites*, 173-184. Oxford: Archaeopress.

Tanasi, D. and Vella, N. 2015. Islands and Mobility: Exploring Bronze Age Connectivity in the South Central Mediterranean. In P. Van Dommelen and A.B. Knapp (eds) *The Cambridge Prehistory of the Bronze and Iron Age Mediterranean*, 57-73. Cambridge: Cambridge University Press.

Tartara, P. 1999. *Torrimpietra*. Florence: Leo S. Olschki.

Tartaron, T. 2018. Geography Matters: Defining Maritime Small Worlds of the Aegean Bronze Age. In J. Leidwanger and C. Knappett (eds) *Maritime Networks in the Ancient Mediterranean World*, 61-92. Cambridge: Cambridge University Press.

Taylor, C. 1979. *Roads and Tracks of Britain*. London: J. M. Dent and Sons Ltd.

Terrell, J.E. 1974. Comparative Study of Human and Lower Animal Biogeography In The Solomon Islands. *Solomon Island Studies in Human Biogeography* 3.

Terrell, J.E. 1977. Human Biogeography in the Solomon Islands. *Fieldiana Anthropology* 68(1): 1-47.

Terrell, J.E. 1986. *Prehistory in the Pacific Islands*. Cambridge: Cambridge University Press.

Terrell, J.E. 2002. Tropical Agroforestry, Coastal Lagoons, and Holocene Prehistory in Greater Near Oceania. In S. Yoshida and P. J. Matthews (eds) *Vegeculture in Eastern Asia and Oceania*, 195-216. Osaka: Japan Centre for Area Studies, National Museum of Ethnology.

Terrell, J.E. 2004. The 'Sleeping Giant' Hypothesis and New Guinea's Place in the Prehistory of Greater Near Oceania. *World Archaeology* 36(4): 601-609.

Terrell, J.E. 2014. Understanding Lapita as History. In E. E. Cochrane and T. Hunt (eds) *The Oxford Handbook of Prehistoric Oceania*, 112-132. Oxford: Oxford University Press.

Terrell, J.E. 2018. Dynamic Network Analysis. 10. What? *Science Dialogues Archive. Integrating Science and the Modern World.* Available at https://toksave.com/tag/archaeology/ (last accessed 11/01/2021)

Terrell, J.E., Hunt, T.L. and Gosden, C. 1997. The Dimensions of Social Life in the Pacific: Human Diversity and the Myth of the Primitive Isolate. *Current Anthropology* 38(2): 155-195.

Terrell, J.E., Shafie, T. and Golitko, M. 2014. How Networks are Revolutionizing Scientific (and maybe Human) Thought. *Scientific American Guest Blog* (https://blogs.scientificamerican.com/guest-blog/how-networks-are-revolutionizing-scientific-and-maybe-human-thought/, accessed 27/10/2020).

Thaler, U. 2005. Narrative and Syntax: New Perspectives on the Late Bronze Age Palace of Pylos, Greece. In A. van Nes (ed.) *5th International Space Syntax Symposium Proceedings*, 323-339. West Lafayette and Ashland: Purdue University Press and AtlasBooks.

Thornton, J. 2001. The Origins and Early History of the Kingdom of Kongo, c. 1350 – 1550. *The International Journal of African Historical Studies* 34(1): 89 – 120.

Tilley, C.Y. 1994. *A Phenomenology of Landscape: Places, Paths, and Monuments (Explorations in Anthropology)*. Oxford: Berg.

Torrence, R., Swadling, P., Kononenko, N., Ambrose, W., Rath, P., Glascock, M.D. 2009. Mid-Holocene Social Interaction in Melanesia: New Evidence from Hammer-Dressed Obsidian Stemmed Tools. *Asian Perspectives* 48(1): 119-148.

Torrence, R., Kelloway, S. and White, P. 2013. Stemmed Tools, Social Interaction, and Voyaging in Early-Mid Holocene Papua New Guinea. *The Journal of Island and Coastal Archaeology* 8(2): 278-310.

Torrence, R. and Swadling, P. 2008. Social Networks and the Spread of Lapita. *Antiquity* 82: 600-616.

Torrence, R. and Victor, K.L. 1995. The Relativity of Density. *Archaeology in Oceania* 30(3): 121-131.

Trappmann, M., Hummell, H.J. and Sodeur, W. 2011. *Strukturanalyse sozialer Netzwerke: Konzepte, Modelle, Methoden* 2., überarb. Aufl. Wiesbaden: VS Verl. für Sozialwiss.

Trombold, C.D. (ed.) 2011. *Ancient Road Networks and Settlement Hierarchies in the New World.* Cambridge: Cambridge University Press.

Tuppi, J. 2014. Approaching Road-Cutting as Instruments of Early Urbanization in Central Tyrrhenian Italy. *Papers of the British School at Rome* 82: 41-74.

Turner, A., Doxa, M., O'Sullivan, D. and Penn, A. 2001. From Isovists to Visibility Graphs: A Methodology for the Analysis of Architectural Space. *Environment and Planning B: Planning and Design* 28(1): 103-121.

Turner, A., Penn, A. and Hillier, B. 2005. An Algorithmic Definition of the Axial Map. *Environment and Planning B: Planning and Design* 32(3): 425-444.

Tusa, S. 1983. *La Sicilia nella preistoria.* Palermo: Sellerio.

Tusa, S. 2004. La Sicilia. Gli Insediamenti. In D. Cocchi Genick (ed.) *L'Età del Bronzo Recente in Italia. Atti del Congresso Nazionale di Lido di Camaiore, 26 – 29 Ottobre 2000*, 327-334. Viareggio.

Tusa, S. 2016. *Primo Mediterraneo. Meditazioni sul mare più antico della storia*. Ragusa: Edizioni di storia e studi sociali.

Usai, A., Schiavo, L. and Fulvia. 2009. Contatti e Scambi. In *Atti della XLIV Riunione Scientifica dell'Istituto Italiano di Preistoria e Protostoria, La Preistoria e la Protostoria della Sardegna. Cagliari, Barumini, Sassari 23 – 28 Novembre 2009*, 271-286. Firenze.

Vagnetti, L., Lo Schiavo, F. 1989. Late Bronze Age Long Distance Trade in the Mediterranean: The Role of the Cypriots. In E. Peltenburg (ed.) *Early Society in Cyprus*, 217-43. Edinburgh: Edinburgh University Press.

Van Dommelen, P. 2016. Classical Connections and Mediterranean Practices: Exploring Connectivity and Local Interactions. In T. Hodos (ed) *The Routledge Handbook of Archaeology and Globalization*, 618-33. London: Routledge.

Van Dommelen, P. and Rowlands, M.J. 2012. Material concerns and colonial encounters, in J. Maran and P. Stockhammer (eds) *Materiality and Social Practice: Transformative Capacities of Intercultural Encounters*, 20-31. Oxford; Oakville, Conn.: Oxbow Books.

Van Nes, A. (ed.) 2005. *5th International Space Syntax Symposium Proceedings*. West Lafayette and Ashland: Purdue University Press and AtlasBooks Distribution.

Van Nes, A. 2014. Indicating Street Vitality in Excavated Towns. Spatial Configurative Analyses Applied to Pompeii. In E. Paliou, U. Lieberwirth and S. Polla (eds) *Spatial Analysis and Social Spaces*, 277-296. Berlin: De Gruyter.

Van Wijngaarden, G.J. 2002. *Use and Appreciation of Mycenaean Pottery in the Levant, Cyprus and Italy (1600-1200 BC)*. Amsterdam: Amsterdam University Press.

Vendramini, F. 1984. *Note sul collaborazionismo bellunese durante l'occupazione tedesca (1943-1945)*. In F. Vendramini (ed.) *Tedeschi, Partigiani e Popolazioni nell'Alpenvorland,* 171-208. Venice: Marsilio Editori.

Verhagen, F. 2015. Peer Polity Interaction in Archaic Latium Vetus: Temple Building as a Form of Competition. *Tijdschrift voor Mediterrane Archeologie* 53: 16-21.

Verhagen, P. (ed.) 2019. *Finding the Limits of the Limes. Modelling Demography, Economy and Transport on the Edge of the Roman Empire*. Cham: Springer.

Vianello, A. 2005. *Late Bronze Age Mycenaean and Italic Products in the West Mediterranean: a Social and Economic Analysis*. Oxford: Archeopress.

Vianello, A. 2009. Late Bronze Age Exchange Networks in the Western Mediterranean. In C. Bachhuber and R. Gareth Roberts (eds) *Forces of Transformation. The End of the Bronze Age in the Mediterranean*, 44-50. Oxford: Oxbow Books.

Volchenkov, D. and Blanchard, P. 2008. City Space Syntax as a Complex Network. Available at: https://arxiv.org/abs/0709.4356.

Voza, G. 1972. Thapsos: Resoconto sulle campagne di scavo del 1970 – 71. In *Atti XV Riunione scientifica IIPP*, 133-157. Istituto Italiano di Preistoria e Protostoria.

Voza, G. 1973. Thapsos, primi risultati delle più recenti ricerche. In *Atti XIV Riunione Scientifica IIPP*, 175-205. Istituto Italiano di Preistoria e Protostoria.

Vragović, I. 2005. Efficiency of Informational Transfer in Regular and Complex Networks. *Physical Review E*. http://journals.aps.org/pre/abstract/10.1103/PhysRevE.1171.036122.

de Vries, J. 1984. *European Urbanization 1500-1800*. Cambridge, Mass.: Harvard Univ. Press.

Walker, H.A. et al. 2000. Network Exchange Theory: Recent Developments and New Directions. *Social Psychology Quarterly* 63(4): 324-337.

Wallace, S. 2018. *Travellers in Time: Imagining Movement in the Ancient Aegean World.* London: Abingdon.

Wallerstein, I. 1974. *The Modern World-System I: Capitalist Agriculture and the Origins of the European World-Economy in the Sixteenth Century.* 1st ed. Academic Press Inc.

Wasserman, S. 1994. *Social Network Analysis: Methods And Applications. Structural Analysis in the Social Sciences.* Cambridge: Cambridge University Press.

Waterton, E. and Watson, S. 2010. Introduction. In E. Waterton and S. Watson (eds) *Culture, Heritage and Representation*, 1-18. Surrey: Ashgate Publishing Ltd.

Watts, D.J. and Strogatz, S.H. 1988. Collective Dynamics of 'Small-World' Networks. *Nature* 393: 440-442.

Waugh, D. 2000. *Geography. An Integrated Approach.* Cheltenham: Nelson Thornes.

Wehner, D. and Wesse, A. (eds) 2015. *Rasthäuser – Gasthäuser – Geschäftshäuser: Zur historischen Archäologie von Wirtshäusern.* Bonn: Habelt.

White, D.A. and Surface-Evans, S.L. (eds) 2012. *Least Cost Analysis of Social Landscapes: Archaeological Case Studies.* Salt Lake City: University of Utah Press.

White, H.C. 2008. *Identity and Control: How Social Formations Emerge.* Princeton: Princeton University Press.

White, J.P. 1996. Rocks in the Head: Thinking about the Distribution of Obsidian in Near Oceania. In J. M. Davidson, G. J. Irwin, B. F. Leach, A. Pawley, and D. Brown (eds) *Oceanic Culture History: Essays in Honour of Roger Green*, 211-224. *New Zealand Journal of Archaeology Special Publication.* Dunedin: New Zealand Journal of Archaeology.

White, R. 1991. *The Middle Ground: Indians, Empires, and Republics in the Great Lakes region, 1650 – 1815.* Studies in American Indian History. New York: Cambridge University Press.

Whitehouse, A.J.O., Maybery, M.T. and Durkin, K. 2006. The Development of the Picture-Superiority Effect. *British Journal of Developmental Psychology* 24: 767-773.

Whittle, A. 2003. *The Archaeology of People: Dimensions of Neolithic Life.* London: Routledge.

Wilkinson, T.C., Sherratt, E.S. and Bennet, J. 2011. *Interweaving Worlds : Systemic Interactions in Eurasia, 7th to the 1st millennia BC.* Oxford: Oxbow Books.

Williams, R. 1977. *Marxism and Literature.* Oxford: Oxford University Press.

Witcomb, A. 2003. *Re-imagining the Museum: Beyond the Mausoleum.* London and New York: Routledge.

Wolf, E.R. 2010. *Europe and the People without History.* Berkeley; London: University of California Press.

Wolpe, H. 1980. *Articulation of Modes of Production: Essays from Economy and Society.* London; Boston: Routledge, Kegan and Paul.

Wood, E. and Latham, K. 2009. Object Knowledge: Researching Objects in the Museum Experience. *Reconstruction* 9(1). Available at: http://digitalcommons.kent.edu/slispubs/53.

Wright, E.O. 2000. *Class Counts.* Cambridge and New York: Cambridge University Press.

Zifferero, A. 1995. Economia Divinità e Frontiere: Sul ruolo di alcuni santuari di confine in Etruria meridionale. *Ostraka. Rivista di Antichità* 4: 333-350.

Zintl, L. 1993. *Der Schöne Brunnen in Nürnberg und seine Figuren: Geschichte und Bedeutung eines Kunstwerkes.* Nürnberg: Hofmann.